A *Step by Step* Approach to World Peace

Region by Region

TED DUNN

Until the various countries of the world get on their feet and become self-supporting there can be no political or economic stability in the world and no lasting peace or prosperity for any of us.
Dean Acheson, Under-Secretary of State in the USA government of 1947 in a speech anticipating the Marshall Plan.

Gooday Publishers

To my wife, my sons and their families

First Published by Gooday Publishers
P.O. Box 60, East Wittering, West Sussex PO20 8RA
in 1988

British Library Cataloguing in Publication Data

Dunn, Ted
   A step by step approach to world peace:
   region by region: a proposal for world peace
   through regional peace and development programmes.
   1. War & peace
   I. Title
   327.1

ISBN 1−870568−11−7

Edited by the same author:
   Alternatives to War and Violence
   Foundations of Peace and Freedom

Typeset in Times by Woodfield Graphics, Fontwell, West Sussex.
Printed in Great Britain by Hollen Street Press, Slough, Berks.

Foreword

In his introduction to the epic report, *North-South*, Willy Brandt recalled an African leader who had invited his Commission to 'contribute to the development of worldwide moral values'. Each further discussion of issues about hunger, the environment, freedom and peace emphasises again how none of them can be approached in isolation. There can be no solutions until humanity has learned the meaning of words like co-operation, unselfishness, fraternity and trust. And if agreement can be attained on moral standards, to the point where they can be embodied in a global system of enforceable law, we are in business.

This was the theme of Mr. Dunn's exciting symposium, *Foundations of Peace and Freedom*, published in 1975. This new study is based on the thesis that agreement on values and purposes is more likely to be achieved at regional level, among peoples of a broadly similar cultural background and experience, than globally. So we may put together a future for Mankind brick by brick.

As a model, he begins with the Marshall Plan to regenerate the shattered Europe of 1947 on a regional basis, with material assistance from a wealthier region. Indeed that initiative led later to such common ventures as the European Convention on Human Rights and the EEC.

Even in Europe their experience has not always been encouraging. Perhaps the human race is beset by problems which it lacks the moral capital to resolve. Perhaps we are doomed. But if there is hope, it lies in the imagination and faith of latter day prophets like this author. If Ted Dunn is wasting his time, then we are lost.

Peter Archer, QC, MP
House of Commons 1988

Commendations

Once more we all owe Ted Dunn a debt of gratitude for another book in which his international vision is grounded in regional reality.

At a time when there is some hope that there may be a small start on the reduction of the nuclear arsenals of the world it is even more important that disarmers should look to the wider horizon. The regional approach is a practical one and in Europe some steps have already been taken. The proposal that there should be an international criminal court is vital if international law is to have the respect it merits and the effectiveness which we, as world citizens, need. This is a useful book which comes at just the right time.

Bruce Kent

Ted Dunn is one of our most original thinkers and persistent workers for world peace. His new proposals affirm that the best way to real peace is by working together for those in need, that this will be achieved through regional developments, and that offenders against human rights should personally face an international court. These important proposals could make UN more effective, and should be widely discussed and pressed home.

John Ferguson

Acknowledgements

I must first thank my wife for all her patience and help over a long period of time. Also to my sons Mark, Alan and Stewart for their help in many ways, especially teaching me to use a word processor and their generous financial contributions. Special thanks must be extended to Bob Garrad and John Cole for their many helpful suggestions when the book was in draft form: also, to William Apps for his invaluable co-operation as co-author of the Proposal, as outlined in the booklet *World Peace Through Regional Peace Development*, a study which provided the basic outline for this book. I am particularly grateful to Colchester and Coggeshall Monthly Meeting of the Religious Society of Friends, and its members, especially its Peace Committee, for supporting this Proposal.

I owe a debt of gratitude to all those MP's, and many other eminent people who responded so encouragingly following the distribution of the booklet, and for the letters of support sent to me by several Commonwealth governments and the Commonwealth Secretariat. Also for the co-operation of those who have generously written the forewords and commendations.

My thanks must be extended to those who organized and led the Quaker Seminar in Strasbourg, in which I participated, about the work of the Council of Europe; to the Quakers in Geneva for arranging for me to meet key UN personnel in the Palais des Nations. All these meetings provided invaluable information and confirmed by belief that peace and security can be attained based on regional co-operation, justice and human rights.

Without the support and co-operation of all the above this work would have been impossible and could not have been brought to a satisfactory conclusion.

Grateful acknowledgements are also made to the following:
The European Organization for Economic Co-operation and Development for permission to use extracts from *Marshall Plan to Global Independence*. Collins the Publishers, for permission to use an extract from the book *Truman* by Roy Jenkins. Ivan Luard for permission to use a letter to me, when he was Parliamentary Secretary of State in 1977. The Guardian for permission to use several articles. Penguin Books for permission to use material from *Debt and Danger* by Lord Lever and Christopher Huhme. The Commonwealth Secretariat for permission to use extracts from the *Nassau Communiqué* following the Commonwealth Heads of Government Meeting in October 1985. The Council of Europe for the use of extracts from their journal FORUM. Hutchinson's the publishers for permission to use an extract from the book *Alfred Russel Wallace* by Harry Clements. Oxfam for permission to use a quotation from *The Poverty of Diplomacy* by David Bull. Oxford University for permission to use work from *The Lawful Rights of Mankind* by Paul Sieghart. Sean MacBride for permission to use extracts from his chapter *Human Rights and the Rule of Law*. Mr F. Nicora, the Directorate-General for Development of the Commission of the European Communities, for permission to use a letter sent to me. The Quaker Council for European Affairs for permission to use their Statement, *Our Vision of Europe*.

Contents

Contents of Appendix

The extracts below are used with their publishers' permission.

Regional Development

International Law and Courts of Law.

The Council of Europe

Other Subjects

Introduction

Forty one years ago, on June 5th 1947, one of the most historic speeches of all time was made by the US Secretary of State, George Marshall, when he outlined his ideas for reconstructing a devastated Europe after the 1939−45 war.[1] The Marshall Plan which followed within a matter of months proved to be a most imaginative, exciting, and visionary idea and was a total success, not only in helping the reconstruction of Western Europe but, perhaps more importantly, in promoting a sense of unity and friendship amongst European nations not previously enjoyed for centuries. The principles which inspired the Marshall Plan and the manner in which it was administered are applicable to the many problems of the regions of the world today, yet they are ignored just at a time when they are most relevant.[2]

Today there is the added advantage of having the United Nations organization under whose auspices regional programmes could be initiated along the lines advocated in this Proposal. Alternatively, the idea could be launched by the Commonwealth, or by Britain and one or two other of the richer nations, in the same manner as the US launched the Marshall Plan. We need an urgent initiative not only to help overcome the poverty in many parts of the world, but also to set a course for peace. Peace is the most urgent issue in the world today yet we lack a positive approach to the challenge. Integrated regional peace and development programmes could be the answer.

The urgent need is for a new UN agency charged with the specific task of reconciling regional conflicts by financing long-term permanent development programmes based on social, economic and

---

1. See page 102
 2. See pages 102−123

1

political human rights. This work demands a totally new approach; instead of seeking solutions to the problems of peace and poverty as separate issues they should be brought together within an integrated concept involving a region. Each nation cannot live in isolation from its neighbour and therefore, if development programmes are to be effective, they must be designed for the region as a whole, based on sound ecological principles, recognising that either we live in harmony with our environment or we perish. To meet this demand it is proposed that a new UN agency be founded called the UN Peace and Development fund charged with the specific task of encouraging Regional Peace and Development Programmes.

Two principles are deemed to be essential. Firstly, development programmes must be based on regions. Secondly, development programmes must integrate social, economic and political justice, based on human rights, within an agreed Code of Agreement.[3] A Code of Agreement is the key to success because without it there can be no assurance that the objectives of peace and development will be achieved. The Code would be an agreement between the proposed UN Peace and Development Fund and representatives from the nations in the region in accordance with the region's aspirations for justice, peace and prosperity and in conformity with the UN Declaration of Human Rights. The Code would also give assurances that these aims would be met and the money not misused by inappropriate development or maladministration. Five requirements are seen as essential for success:

(i)   The appointment of a Regional Secretariat to administer and monitor, in co-operation with the states in the region, a development programme in accordance with the Code of Agreement;

(ii)   Agreement about the nature of 'development', i.e. land reform, self-sufficiency, permanency, water supply, tree planting.

(iii) Determination on the part of the nations *within* the region to resolve their differences peacefully, and subsequently to commence a disarmament programme;

(iv)   Determination by the region to become a region of peace by requesting the Great Powers to respect the neutrality of the region;

(v)   Establishment within the region of a Regional Court of Human Rights similar to the European Court of Human Rights.

---

3. See chapter on 'Code of Agreement', page 19

Responsibility for initiating a regional peace and development pro-gramme would rest solely with the developing countries. They would ask for help knowing in advance the general outline of the Code of Agreement.

It is suggested the development programme be spread over a 5 – 10 year period. If during this time the spirit of the agreement were to be violated, the proposed UN Peace and Development Fund would reserve the right to stop all further aid.

The rich nations for their part would commit themselves to establish the region on a sound economic foundation by providing funds on a scale similar to those which enabled the Marshall Plan to help Europe to recover from the devastation of the Second World War.

It is suggested that the first regional peace and development pro-gramme should be undertaken in one of the smaller regions of the world. A small region could be helped with less cost and difficulty than a large one, thus enabling an early start to be made and valuable experience to be gained in the near future. It is important to demon-strate by experience the practical nature of a proposal so essential if further funds are to be found for more ambitious regional development programmes.

The principles in a Code of Agreement would be widely known by all regions before they applied for development aid but the details could be negotiated. Consequently only those regions willing to accept the disciplines of the Code of Agreement would apply thus assuring those nations providing the funds that their money would be well spent achieving the aims and purpose of peace and development.

Nor should the problem about what constitutes a region be too difficult to decide because regions form themselves naturally according to circumstances far too varied to be ordered from outside the region. A region therefore may be as small as a divided island or as large as half a continent. Thus it is possible to have a region within a region. Regions could also overlap and through co-operation become a larger region. This process of co-operation would encourage global co-operation within the UN. The urge to co-operate must come from local level and proceed to world level. Regional Peace and Development Programmes could encourage this urge by providing the necessary structure and incentive for co-operation.

Since the UN was founded at the end of the 1939 – 45 war its many agencies have gained a tremendous amount of valuable knowledge and experience in almost every human endeavour, but because this expertise has lacked an adequate structure to integrate social and economic issues within a political context, the potential of the programmes launched under UN auspices has not been achieved. The reason is clear: UN development programmes are usually given to individual countries, seldom on a regional basis, and never as an integrated concept as suggested in this Proposal. Nor does the UN have the necessary organisation to encourage such a process. The UN Development Programme, the World Bank and the International Monetory Fund are increasingly supporting regional initiatives, but they do not work within a comprehensive regional concept similar to that envisaged in the Code of Agreement. Aid is not granted on a scale similar to the Marshall Plan or regions required to become peaceful or human rights respected. Aid is also invariably tied to capital investments and to inappropriate technology. Most so called 'aid' is also 'given' in loan form with the crazy result that today the rich nations are receiving back from the poor countries more than they are 'giving' to them! 'Real Aid' on the other hand should seek to promote the basic wealth of a region and this usually means encouraging projects for which there is no direct benefit to the countries providing the funds such as relevant education, land reform, tree planting, water supplies etc. It also means helping those in most need, not only for humanitarian reasons but as the best means of promoting wealth and peaceful relationships.

The problems facing us today are fundamentally psychological and philosophical in nature and one answer is to be found in the age old concept of Natural Law as discussed in later chapters. Until we learn to live in harmony with our environment by encouraging favourable social and economic conditions within a structure of political organization which supports these aims, we will continue to fail and lapse into conflict. Thus there is the need for a new UN agency to overcome these problems and a UN Peace and Development Fund to finance the Regional Peace and Development Programmes is therefore proposed.

For many years there has been mounting criticism of the UN being 'top heavy' and a recent UN Report[4] indicates that 70% of UN resources goes into this work. An integrated regional concept co-ordinating all UN work in a region, administered by a small

---

4. See Appendix on page 117

4

Regional Secretariat, could overcome this problem and save large sums of money.

Further large sums of money could be saved by the region itself once the beneficial effects of regional co-operation made itself felt. Expenditure on armaments in the Third World has increased very fast in recent years and this process could be reversed.

The problem of financing Regional Peace and Development Programmes is considered in greater detail in a later chapter but the main source of income must depend on generating the political will in the richer world. This can be created by recognising that we all live in one world and that what affects any part affects us all. For our own security therefore it is essential that we encourage Regional Peace and Development Programmes by all means possible. If we can also demonstrate that this approach to our security is far, far more cost effective than reliance on expensive armaments then there is hope that the many UN conferences proposing the transfer of funds from armaments to development will succeed. [5]

Law, especially international law, cannot be enforced by violence but must be nurtured by supporting those conditions which give individuals and communities a sense of meaning, purpose and the means to live fulfilled lives. Only then will the forces of international law work for the common good, as exemplified in post-war Europe.

Regional Peace and Development Programmes should be considered as a trigger mechanism to enable rich and poor countries alike to be freed from the burden of armaments and war, probably the main cause of poverty around the world.[6]

Money to finance Regional Peace and Development Programmes could also be found if political will were generated, similar to that which initiated the Marshall Plan for Western Europe. Regional programmes would be more cost effective, and more certain to achieve their objectives than development programmes as at present conceived. If, in addition, governments learnt to appreciate that regional development programmes are the best way of promoting their own security, freedom and prosperity, finding adequate funds should present less difficulty. Enlightened self-interest for the poor countries could

---

5. See chapter 'World Security'.
6. For examples of proposals submitted by governments to the UN to help finance development programmes, see page 30

prove to be the means by which our own peace and security can be achieved.[7]

The immediate objective of Regional Peace and Development Programmes is to promote peace and development in the regions, especially those regions suffering appalling poverty and deprivation of human rights, but the ultimate objective must be world peace. This objective could be achieved by promoting an environment in the regions which encourages and nurtures social and economic justice and law based on the *UN Declaration of Human Rights*. These Rights could be enforced in the regions in a manner similar to the European Court of Human Rights. To make international law really effective, however, we need to encourage our governments to promote the idea of a Commissioner for Human Rights and an International Criminal Tribunal to which individuals who commit crimes may be taken. Only then will we have a truly effective alternative to war. Seeking the social, economic and political basis of law and the machinery for its enforcement at both regional and global levels is therefore seen as the underlying theme of this book.

History of the Proposal

The Proposal for World Peace through Regional Peace and Development Programmes was first published as a small booklet in 1983; since then it has aroused considerable support from individuals involved in government and international organizations.

The Proposal has had a long gestation period and can be dated from the early 1960s when the peace marches to Aldermaston began. It was argued then that to protest only against the evils of war, especially the nuclear bomb, did little to remove the public's fears of a possible aggressor and that the peace movement's first priority should be to search for an alternative to war to maintain our freedoms and our security. Without an adequate alternative, fear will encourage most people to support a so-called 'defence' policy. The peace movement has relied for too long on the horrors of nuclear war as a means of encouraging people to support nuclear disarmament. Fear has its rightful place in acting as a spur to action but fear without belief and knowledge in an alternative leads only to frustration and impotence in

---

7. See the chapter Financing Regional Peace and Development Programmes on page 30

the face of today's many problems, of which war is its ultimate manifestation. Only a positive, creative approach to the problem can resolve these difficulties supported by sound evidence that there is a workable alternative to war. Such evidence was indicated by the success of the Marshall Plan. We should build on this example.

The search for alternatives to war and violence in the 1960s was sought through resolutions at several conferences. Unfortunately the standard reaction to requests for peace research at various peace gatherings was dismissive, the argument being that it would be too ambitious, or too divisive, and that it was more important to campaign single-mindedly against the bomb. What failed to be appreciated was that a positive alternative to war would complement the campaign for nuclear disarmament. As a result the peace movement has lost many years of opportunity to put its house in order. Even now, despite much good work and gathering interest in peace research, the peace movement has still not yet formulated a positive approach to peace, such as put forward in this Proposal. The Movement seems content to campaign against war without having a clear conception about what it is campaigning for.

This lack of research into understanding the alternatives to war and violence led several of us to organise a conference on the subject in 1961, supported by Colchester Quakers and branches of the United Nations Association, CND, the Fellowship of Reconciliation and the Anglican Pacifist Fellowship. The success of this conference, in which over 200 people took part confirmed my belief that there was a desperate need for more research into the principles of creating a peaceful world. As a result of this interest a Publications Committee was formed to invite well-known Sponsors and Editorial Advisers to help assemble a collection of essays by eminent writers, each an authority on his subject dealing with as many alternatives to war and violence as possible. The result was the book *Alternatives to War and Violence*. This work led to a deeper understanding of the natural laws which make for peace such as learning the importance of structures, of education and co-operation; and seeking specific examples of how to maintain the peace without recourse to violence. The outcome of this search was a second book, with a similar format, called *Foundations of Peace and Freedom*. This won the World Education Award for 1976 as, 'the book which has made the greatest contribution towards promoting the social purposes of education'.[8]

7

Several years later, with the ending of the Vietnam war and the tragic episode of the Boat People engaging public concern, it was felt that the wave of public sympathy and generosity provided an opportunity to encourage the British government to take the initiative at the UN to provide funds adequate to help reconstruct Vietnam and Cambodia. The belief was held that this solution would be less costly in the long run than allowing the region to remain in dire poverty, possibly cheaper than rehabilitating the Vietnamese in countries around the world. Concern was also felt for the people of the region considering the fact that Britain had supported the Vietnam war, in which more bombs were dropped on innocent people than throughout the 1939−45 war. Consequently it was felt then there was a possibility that the public's generosity being shown towards the Boat People could be extended to encourage the government to respond by an act of goodwill similar to that which promoted the Marshall Plan, when the USA gave over 2% of its Gross National Product to a West European Development Programme. (other estimates put this figure as high as 4%) In addition, it was thought a regional development programme for Vietnam and its neighbours would make good economic sense as an act of enlightened self interest. As recipients of Marshall Aid the least the British can do is repay the debt by using our present wealth to aid a region in a far more desperate state than we were in 1945.[9]

The outcome of this concern for Vietnam and Cambodia led to a letter being sent to *The Friend*, the Quaker weekly, suggesting a Study Group be formed to consider what initiative could be taken to encourage a development programme for Vietnam and Cambodia. This resulted in a series of meetings with representatives from national charities to see if anything could be done. Unfortunately, despite a letter in *The Times* from the Chairman of Quaker Peace and Service this concern fell on stony ground, mainly because the wave of public concern evaporated, discouraged possibly by USA pressure to stop all aid to Vietnam.

Although the idea failed, the experience of discussing the problems of Vietnam with people with first-hand knowledge of the area and expert knowledge of development programmes, was invaluable. It confirmed my belief that sending aid to a developing country without at the same

---

8. See Bibliography
9. See Marshall's speech on page 102

time integrating the deeper underlying social, economic, and political problems on a regional basis could never provide a lasting solution.

It was about this time that the Falklands conflict brutally demonstrated once again the need for an alternative to war at a time when the British government was pouring billions of pounds into the Falkland Islands to make it into a 'Fortress'. If only this money could have been made available for initiating a South American Regional Peace and Development Programme who knows what a difference this could have made to the security of the Falklanders and to the peace and development prospects of Argentinia and Chile, not to mention its effect on resolving the financial debts, which the instability of the region and indeed the world economy incurred.[10]

Gradually the ideas resulting from the research undertaken for the two books mentioned above fell into place and thanks to the support of Colchester Quakers and very helpful collaboration with William Apps, a small booklet entitled *Proposal for World Peace Through Regional Peace and Development Programmes* was published in 1985 with Commendations from many prominent individuals. This Proposal was widely circulated and has received considerable support in political circles as an idea with immediate application to today's international problems. This support has encouraged me to research the subject further and is the justification for this book.

More About The Proposal

Despite the reservations by some critics about the motives behind the Marshall Plan, the folly of demanding reparations from Germany after the Second World War was averted. Social and economic conditions after the First World War led directly to the impoverishment of Germany and the rise of Hitler, while conditions after the Second World War, thanks to the Marshall Plan, led to Europe's recovery and enemies became friends; it seemed that we had learned the lesson that, while retribution creates the ideal breeding ground for extremist governments, a positive, creative, and generous response based on a regional development programme heals the wounds of war and promotes peaceful relationships. This remarkable contrast in the treatment

---

10. See the chapter 'Which Regions' on page 54

of our enemies following two world wars confirmed my belief that injustice breeds injustice and that justice encourages peaceful relationships. The Marshall Plan helped us to avoid repeating the mistakes of 1918 and led to the rehabilitation of Germany within a regional development programme. The Proposal for Regional Peace and Development Programmes is, therefore, based on a practical working model and should be applied to other regions of the world.

The Marshall Plan was, however, initiated in only ten months in exceptional circumstances immediately after the war, and before the UN was formed. Since then the UN, through its many agencies, has gained vast experience in many fields of international co-operation, but because the nations of the world have refused to give it the support it needs, it is generally perceived as being a failure and in desperate need of reform. But the reform of an organisation as large and cumbersome as the UN is a major undertaking because too many vital interests are involved. If, however, it were to be approached in the manner advocated in this Proposal gradual reform of the UN could be achieved without requiring changes in its constitution or provoking controversial policy decisions. Evolutionary change of the UN, within a long-term vision of its future as envisaged in later chapters, provides probably our best hope for the peace of the world. [11]

By basing the Proposal firmly on the *UN Universal Declaration of Human Rights*, the establishment of regional courts of law, similar to the European Court of Human Rights, would be encouraged. This would mean the nations within each region sacrificing a small degree of sovereignty, the essential prerequisite for peace between nations.

Regional law must be seen as a protection for the individual, not as a threat. Freedom under the law can only become a reality if the government itself is under the law in accordance with the dictum enunciated by Bracton, the great lawyer in the thirteenth century, when he said:

> the King ought not to be under any man, but he ought to be under God and the law, since the law makes the King. Therefore let the King render unto the law what the law has rendered unto the King, namely dominion and power; for there is no king where will prevails and not the law. (from D.V. Cowen's book, *The Foundations of Freedom* Oxford University Press 1961)

---

11. See the chapter 'The Future of the UN' on page 40

This idea requires that if a king or government is to be given the authority to make laws, this authority will only be given if the king or government rules according to a sense of justice tempered by mercy and is itself under the law. Consequently it is important for the powers of government to be separate and independent from the judiciary and the executive. It is an idea vitally important for the administration of justice and conforms to the philosophy of Natural Law.[12] Each arm of government must act as a restraint on the other to ensure that law is upheld impartially and to prevent power being wrongfully accumulated or in the case of international relationships, to prevent a dictatorship by a majority at the expense of a minority for its own selfish ends. Democracy must respect minorities, with minorities and majorities agreeing about what constitutes the nature of justice and basic human rights. A democracy which denies minorities their human rights soon degenerates into a tyranny. On the other hand a king, or government which respects the law gains the allegiance of the people. Regional Peace and Development Programmes would seek to encourage this process. Fortunately international law has already been formulated in the *UN Universal Declaration of Human Rights* and the *Nuremberg Principles*[13] and therefore the task before us is to establish the machinery for their enforcement, not only in political terms but equally, possibly more importantly, in social and economic terms. Law without the support and co-operation of the people is a recipe for a ruthless tyranny or lawlessness. Only law based on consent, justice, fairness and co-operation can succeed and create the kind of environment in which peaceful relationships may become the natural order of the day.

The proposed UN Peace and Development Fund would seek interdependent solutions to regional problems and would be administered by a Secretariat of experts following the example of the Organization for European Economic Co-operation under the Marshall Plan. It is also suggested that instead of the help being given in loan form to individual countries it should be given in grant form to a region over a limited period of between 5 and 10 years. After such time the region should be more self-sufficient with a healthy economy: independent, and able to play its full part in the deliberations of the UN by encouraging global ideas

---

12. See the chapter 'The Nature of Law' on page 89
13. See page 112

such as the World Economic Programme or an International Criminal Tribunal.[14] When social, economic, and political justice is available to all at the regional level, and a favourable climate of opinion is created, the region can become stable, enjoy peace and a healthy economy at home and play its rightful place in world affairs.

We cannot hope to change the world in the immediate future but we can make an immediate start and proceed step by step, region by region; in the process we could discover a renewed faith and hope in the UN. Indirectly Regional Peace and Development Programmes would promote the basis of law and order upon which our security ultimately depends. The last two chapters of this book dealing with World Security and The Nature of Law seek to understand the relationship between the regions and international law; these are discussed briefly.

THE LONG TERM PROSPECT

Collective Security or International Law?

The idea of Collective Security has dominated many of our most committed peace workers yet it is an idea which is an illusion delaying us from tackling the fundamental social, economic and political problems. It has also stopped us taking realistic measures to reform the UN. [15]

Law, to be effectively implemented, requires two complementary approaches. Firstly, that individuals are made responsible for crimes they commit; secondly, for the individual to have the right to appeal to a regional or international court of human rights against unjust laws. Far more progress has been made in these directions, both in the UN and in Europe, than is generally recognised; for instance, the Nuremberg Principles[16] have already been formulated, following a directive from the UN, and universally recognised as having the force of international law, while the decisions of European Court of Human Rights are binding on the governments in the Council of Europe.[17] These are proven practical ways of enforcing international law without threatening war. On the other hand the task of enforcing international law against a *nation* when that nation is determined not to comply is probably an impossibility, especially if that nation is a great power.[18] But until the

---

14. See page 108: 'The Nuremberg Principles'
15. See chapter 'The Future of the UN' on page 40

12

environmental factors which determine people's behaviour patterns are changed, and economic and social priorities encourage co-operation for everyone's mutual benefit, as envisaged in the Proposal for Regional Peace and Development Programmes, it is doubtful if nations will support the necessary regional and international courts of law to make law effective.

If the attempt is made to enforce law against a state by violence, as envisaged by the concept of Collective Security under the constitution of the UN, the very basis of international law is undermined and trust and confidence, which should form the basis of international law, is destroyed. The concept of Collective Security is, therefore, seen as a recipe for Collective Insecurity, as the experiences in Ethiopia when sanctions were attempted, and in Korea where UN troops were involved, have demonstrated. Only law enforced against *individuals* can be successful; it is impossible by any other means. This concept has a proved record in most, if not all, of the federal states of the world. It is also a universally recognised procedure under national law in most democratic countries. The principle therefore is well established and should be extended to the UN itself.

The achievement of this ideal, however, demands trust and confidence between the forces of law and the general public based on a mutuality of interests. These virtues cannot be ordered but must grow naturally in a healthy environment such as this Proposal seeks to encourage and establish. The Marshall Plan showed the way forward; today we need a similar vision and generosity of spirit. We have nothing to lose but fear itself and everything to gain. There is a tremendous latent force for goodwill in the world which could be harnessed but which we allow to remain dormant because we have lost faith in ourselves. The world urgently needs a new vision and a way out of the desperate state of affairs afflicting us all today. Let us celebrate the 41st anniversary of the Marshall Plan by taking the first step in one of the poor regions of the world. Not only would such a step be the best way of overcoming poverty, tyranny and conflict in a region, but it would also provide the world with a practical working model proving that there is a better way to maintain our own security than the threat of war.

---

16. see page 108
17. See page 114
18. See the last two chapters, pages 73 and 89

Step By Step Towards World Peace

When the UN was formed the universal belief was that peace must be sought on a global scale. Unfortunately experience has taught us that this ideal is too ambitious to be practical politics. Trying to find agreement between well over a hundred different nations on vital issues, and between Great Powers with very different philosophies, is to court disappointment especially when success depends on an integrated and ecological approach to the problem of peace.

Despite this criticism, the UN has laid firm foundations on which to build. We now have a wealth of experience, especially in the UN agencies, which should be harnessed to a new concept encouraging a step by step, region by region approach within a long-term perspective aimed at strengthening international law. Regionalism already has considerable support and many regions have formed their own organizations, but they lack the financial resources for success. There is also no international agency capable of encouraging the necessary structure of organization to make such an idea a reality.

Most regions have also been drawn into a world economic slump which prevents them becoming free, self-sufficient and independent. Great Power politics have led to over a hundred wars since 1945, many of them involving the Great Powers. Trust and confidence between nations has been undermined and the regions impoverished to such an extent that the future of the Third World looks desperate unless they receive help to help themselves. Aid should be given not as a charity but because of enlightened self-interest and moral reasons without expectation of immediate economic gain. Given in this way help would enable suitable development to take place relevant to the

14

needs of the region and would initiate long-term development based on the region's own resources. Aid should not be seen as a crutch but as a means of 'priming the pump' to enable the country to be self-supporting; it would not be given as a permanent yearly handout but a temporary measure to enable the region to become economically and politically independent. Only then will it be in a position to play its full part in the UN assisting in the promotion of more regional peace and development programmes and other measures which can only be adopted on a global scale.

What is needed is not a new controversial change in the constitution of the UN but a new UN agency—a UN Peace and Development Fund—to which any nation could contribute immediately. The Fund would provide generous grants, not loans, over a five to ten year period, paid in yearly instalments to those regions urgently in need, conditional on their continuing to observe an agreed Code of Agreement.[1]

The Code would require:

—a Regional Secretariat to encourage and ensure that the spirit of the Code was implemented;
—an understanding about the nature of development;
—provision for a Regional Court of Human Rights;
—a commitment to seek peaceful relationships in the region;
—a commitment to take positive steps towards disarmament.

The region would also be asked to become a neutral nuclear-free zone, and to support the idea of an International Criminal Tribunal, at the UN, before which individuals who commit crimes, as outlined in the Nuremberg Principles, could be taken. These aims are thought to be in accordance with most Third World aspirations, (for example the African National Congress Declaration) and by UN experts according to UN publications.[2] Details of the Agreement could vary from region to region, but the basic outlines would be the same and known in advance by a region requesting help.

A positive peace policy on the lines of the above proposal, based on the regions of the world, could in some regions be initiated immediately with the same speed and urgency as the Marshall Plan which rescued Europe in 1947. The threat to the world is far greater now and the rich

---

1. See chapter 'Code of Agreement' for details, page 19
2. See page 116

world in a better position to help than it was just after the war. We are willing to spend vast sums on 'defending' peace, why can we not spend some of this wealth 'promoting' peace?

The help would need to be adequate to restore the prosperity of the region, and it should be given through the proposed UN Peace and Development Fund. This would have to command the trust and confidence of the region, and of the donor countries. Again, as with the Regional Secretariat, the independence, ability, and integrity of the personnel administering the UN Fund would be vitally important.

The above Proposal should be founded on the old, neglected but respected concept of Natural Law,[3] founded on social, economic and political justice. Justice alone however is often inadequate if a sense of generosity and fairness is lacking. Development programmes must also be based on a region, not one nation, and within an integrated concept as enshrined in the Universal Declaration of Human Rights.

Development programmes along these lines would make far better use of resources than inappropriate ventures like cash cropping and prestige works. Tree planting, good water supplies, and land reform to encourage individual independence could contribute more to the commonwealth than expensive capital-consuming import-demanding projects. The wealth of the region should be nurtured from the roots and be of a permanent character, not a fragile one based on high technology. There is a wealth of knowledge and expertise available to advise on the most appropriate forms of development. Agreement should be sought between these advisers and the members of the region. Of even greater importance however, is the need to encourage co-operation, concili-ation and reconciliation between nations of the regions. To give aid without ensuring peaceful co-existence within the region is almost a waste of money as the aid, military and economic, given to Ethiopia over many years has demonstrated. Clearly the rich nations must help in times of disaster, but it would be far better and less costly to remove the causes of the disaster at an early stage.

The way in which the Council of Europe developed has shown that if social, economic and political justice is encouraged by a development programme similar to the Marshall Plan, co-operation follows as a natural consequence. The Council of Europe has proved that nations are willing to sacrifice a degree of sovereignty to an independent Regional

---

3. See separate chapter for this important concept, page 89

Court of Human Rights provided there is the necessary degree of trust and confidence, based on justice and fairness between the nations concerned. Regional peace and development programmes could provide the means of achieving these ideals and transform our dependence on defence preparations into security under the rule of law. Gradually the belief that power comes from the barrel of the gun could be replaced by the idea of power arising from moral and natural forces based on the social, economic and political justice ritualized through international courts of law. This power is the only alternative to violence as a means of maintaining peace. It cannot be found overnight but needs nurturing within a well conceived practical organized structure such as this Proposal offers. When progress has been made in this direction disarmament will become possible and the vast resources at present squandered on defence preparation could be made available to promote more ambitious regional peace and development programmes.

The beauty of this Proposal is that a start could be made immediately, with or without the support of the Great Powers. The initiative for a peaceful world could come from Britain tomorrow. The USA introduced the Marshall Plan almost overnight[4] pledging help to lay the foundations of European co-operation. As a result old enemies became friends and the threat of war between members of the Council of Europe was eliminated.

The sceptics may say the Marshall Plan was inspired by self-interested motives but it has provided us with a practical working model proving the viability of this Proposal. We should build on that inspiration by incorporating the idea into the UN. The proposed UN Peace and Development Fund could be initiated by one or more of the richer countries such as Britain, Canada, or Scandinavia, unilaterally donating adequate funds to a small region, possibly the South Pacific Islands, or the Cape Verde Islands; or, more ambitiously, when funds allow, for the Caribbean, the Horn of Africa, Latin America, and S.E. Asia. The idea is also ideal for resolving conflicts in divided countries such as Sri Lanka, or regions like Southern Africa. The urgent need is for a start to be made somewhere, no matter how small. Example is by far the best form of persuasion.

If it proves impossible to work through the UN, a good alternative would be to ask the Commonwealth to initiate the Proposal.

4. See Marshall's speech

The Commonwealth Conference of Prime Ministers in 1985[5] strongly supported the concept of regional development. If the Commonwealth promoted a Commonwealth Peace and Development Fund to initiate Regional Peace and Development Programmes for one of its regions, the Commonwealth would be given a new sense of meaning and purpose. More important, the world would be given a new sense of hope, based on the realization that there is a positive alternative to war which could, step by step, region by region, transform the world. If we build the institutions of peace and security based on social, economic and social justice in the spirit of love and generosity within a viable structure international law and disarmament will follow, but if we insist on putting the cart before the horse by seeking disarmament without resolving social, economic and political problems we must not be surprised if peace remains a dream. A step by step, region by region approach to these problems, within a global context, is seen as the most appropriate means of achieving this goal.

---

5. See page 107

Code of Agreement

A Code of Agreement is seen as the key to success because without it there can be no assurance that the aims and purpose of a peace and development programme would be attained. Experience has demonstrated that development programmes have failed, partly because of being ill-conceived or inappropriate, partly because of maladministration, but mainly because development has not been integrated within a positive peace policy for fear of interfering with a nation's independence. This is a real problem which must be met with sympathy and understanding; unless we can find a way of overcoming this difficulty little long-term good can be achieved.

The reason for this is clear. For instance, a country such as Ethiopia is in desperate need of help, yet (despite substantial assistance given during the past few years) unless Ethiopia's wars with neighbouring states are resolved all the help given can only be palliative, not curative. These wars have been fuelled by the USSR and the USA providing military equipment, with each country attempting to gain a sphere of influence and military bases, with the inevitable result that Ethiopia has been impoverished to the point of exhaustion. Consequently, when drought came the country was ill-prepared. Aid was then poured in to help the starving millions, but with the war continuing the main problem is left untouched. This example could be multiplied in other parts of Africa and elsewhere around the world. It would be so much cheaper, easier and more effective to promote a Regional Peace and Development Programme at a very early stage before a crisis arises.

In cash terms, the cost to the USA and the USSR and other countries, of pouring military equipment into poor countries in support of many of the 150 wars waged since 1945 must be enormous, while the cost to Ethiopia alone, in human and economic terms, has been appalling. In addition, the other nations of the world have responded with large sums of money to promote development and emergency aid. If only a small fraction of all this expenditure had been spent at a much earlier stage, as outlined in this Proposal, all this suffering could have been avoided and the world made a much safer place. Clearly the need is to integrate social and economic problems within a much wider political context.

Unfortunately, there is little real hope of integrating these issues on a regional basis and scale unless large scale financial help is given by the rich world. Recent attempts to promote a Central American Peace Plan agreed by five of their presidents may prove this forecast to be too pessimistic but if they succeed it will be an impressive display of unity in the face of USA hostility. If the money given to the Contras by the USA were to be given instead to support the Central American Peace Plan (an outcome of the Contadora Plan, which in very many respects resembles the Regional Peace and Development Programme put forward in this paper) it is highly probable that a new era of peace and prosperity could be inaugurated in the region. [1]

Unfortunately there is little hope of the USA and the other rich nations providing adequate funds unless there is some real assurance that the money spent will succeed in achieving its objectives of regional peace and development. Somehow or other we must find the language to convince the rich countries that peace is indivisible and that their own country's wellbeing depends equally on the wellbeing of other countries, especially, as in the case with the USA, of regions in its own 'backyard'.

The poorer nations will not accept conditional aid unless the conditions are seen to be fair and just and not merely aimed at enabling a foreign country to impose its will. Trust and confidence in the motives of the donor countries are therefore seen to be essential if the Code of Agreement is to be accepted by the nations involved in a regional project. What makes the Central American Peace Proposal so interesting however, is that it places similar emphasis on the need for human rights, economic development and regional co-operation as this Proposal.

Fortunately there is already wide consensus between all nations, rich and poor, about the nature of such an Agreement. All nations have already given their support to the UN Universal Declaration of

---

1. See the chapter 'Which Regions?' on page 54

Human Rights and there is widespread agreement that human rights must include social and economic justice alongside political rights. There is also universal support for national sovereignty with all nations wanting economic and political independence, free from domination by any one great power. There is also a growing recognition that aid in the past has been inappropriate and often ill-conceived. Agreement too that sound development requires good adminstration. All these points of agreement give us a sound base on which to formulate a Code of Agreement. The following principles are therefore seen as being essential for success:

1. To appoint a Regional Secretariat to initiate and monitor the Code of Agreement

The personnel in the Secretariat should not be composed of politicians but of individuals appointed by the states in the region who can also command the respect, trust and confidence of the UN Peace and Development Fund for their ability and expertise. There is a wealth of talent to be found in the various UN agencies and in the voluntary organizations. The Marshall Plan was agreed between Western Europe and the USA, and implemented by a small Secretariat of independent experts who monitored it in accordance with the agreement. Very little bureaucracy was involved and the actual work of implementing the Plan devolved on to the individual nations of Western Europe, in accordance with the Agreement reached in the Marshall Plan under the supervision of the Secretariat under the chairmanship of Lord Franks.[2]

2. Agreement on the nature of development

This will vary from region to region but there is general recognition that development in the past has too often been inappropriate. It is also acknowledged that much more emphasis must be given to encouraging self-sufficiency and to avoiding dependence on cash crops for export which can so easily be overproduced in a competitive world free trade economy with the disastrous financial results we are witnessing today. This problem is compounded by the fact that hard-won exports all too

---

2. For Lord Franks' speech about the fulfilment of the Marshall Plan, see page 85

frequently go to pay for inappropriate expensive imports. More emphasis should therefore be given to providing basic needs, such as food, housing, education and health locally, all of which can be generated and encouraged without expensive imports. Prestige and glamorous high-technology forms of development have also failed through lack of knowledge or 'back up' facilities. The developing world is beginning painfully to recognise that all that glisters in the West is not gold; that mere money, instead of helping the country to prosperity, all too often reduces it to poverty with huge debts it cannot repay. A country, on the other hand, which has a sound economic base may not be able to afford the same technology as the Western World but its basic needs, of health and education and economic recovery, alongside respect for human dignity and human rights, could lay the foundations for future prosperity.

Fortunately there is a growing understanding about the nature of this problem and also a wealth of knowledge about appropriate development in organizations such as Oxfam and the UN agencies which needs harnessing. The poor nations do not need expensive equipment which demands constant expert maintenance, but they do need financial help to pay wages for projects such as tree planting and better water supplies, education and appropriate medical services. Most people in poor countries would also respond with far better productivity if they were to be given the incentive of owning their own land within a local co-operative. The example of the Nordic Development Programme in Kenya and Tanzania is to be commended, as outlined in the supplement in Development Forum.

The work of the Rome-based International Fund for Agricultural development (IFAD) has also pioneered, during the past 10 years, probably the most efficient and successful multilateral initiative of all international development programmes by giving agricultural credit direct to poor farmers, rather than to governments, and by making agreements with governments conditional on satisfaction of a number of conditions, principally how the ultimate beneficiaries will benefit from the scheme and close supervision and implementation. IFAD is also unique in that the developing countries themselves contribute 40% of the Fund yet have 66% of the vote, thus ensuring that the conditions required are based on motives for their own benefit. The indicators of success are that for an outlay of 2 billion dollars (in loans over 10 years) and co-financing of 6 billion dollars the food deficits of the developing countries are expected to be reduced by 20%. Unfortunately IFAD is facing a financial problem owing to the OPEC countries (its main source of income) not being able to maintain their former support.[3] (This newspaper is published ten times a year by the UN Division for Economic and Social Information and the UN University. It is a mine of information and a splendid example of UN work.)

Financial help would be needed to buy suitable land, and to help co-operatives in their early stages. Land value taxation should also be considered as a means of avoiding the gross inequalities which arise from other forms of taxation and to ensure a more just society. Many people, inspired by writings of Henry George, the great American economist, regard the need for land value taxation as the one essential prerequisite for the rejuvenation of the economies of the poor (and the rich) nations. As all wealth comes from the land as rent or produce, it is the land which should be taxed and proceeds given to the community, not into the hands of the few landowners. To avoid bloody conflict during a period of changeover the landowners would need fair compensation with which Regional Peace and Development Programmes could help.

Financial help is also needed to encourage education: not education to pass Western academic examinations, but education appropriate to the well-being of the country, i.e. agriculture, basic health, literacy and a greater sense of history, values, and reverence for life. The aim should be to encourage wealth to grow from the bottom up in a manner which can be sustained permanently in accordance with local traditions. This will require large sums of money which should be given in grant form in yearly instalments over a period of 5 to 10 years (but minute if compared with defence expenditures). It should be adequate to ensure success during that time, after which the region should be self-supporting and independent.

It is suggested that the example of the great Danish educationalist Bishop Grundtvic, who founded the Scandinavian Folk High Schools, be followed. Grundtvic was born in 1783 and lived through a period when Denmark was in a state of turmoil and poverty not unlike many Third World countries today. Thanks to a belief that education is for living a full creative life, and to his emphasis on values, the Folk High Schools transformed the Scandanavian countries into the most socially

---

3. See *Development Forum*, September 1987

conscious region in the world today with the world's highest standard of living. It is no accident that these countries now give the most help, in GNP terms, to Third World Development Programmes than any of the other countries of the world. Peter Manniche is a modern disciple of Grundtvic, whose ideas are very relevant to today's Third World problems.[4] He has, in more recent years, founded the International Folk High Schools and written about rural development and the changing countries of the world.

Efforts to achieve peace along these lines are probably a hundred, if not a thousand times more cost-effective as a means of preserving and maintaining the peace than military expenditure. Development programmes have the additional advantage of helping to improve the world economic situation and in some instances rescuing a poor country from the huge burden of debt which forces it to adopt an export economy ill-suited to its problems.

Different countries and different regions will of course each need different kinds of development programmes, but unless there is a sound understanding about the nature of the problems facing the countries in the regions of the world, and an educational system established relevant to their own culture and values, little long term good can be achieved no matter how much aid is given. It is a truism that 'no man is an island' and that no country can stand alone; therefore all education should include world citizenship with all that that implies in sharing our wealth and our willingness to support the work of the UN.

3. Agreement is needed between the nations in a region to undertake to resolve any differences peacefully

How they do so would be for the nations themselves to decide. This part of the Code of Agreement would be encouraged by the Regional Secretariat in every way possible; perhaps with help towards building a bridge or railway between states, thus giving the nations the incentive to co-operate and sink their differences for a common purpose. A regional education centre could be promoted, devoted to encouraging understanding between the states in the region and to teaching appropriate technology. UNESCO and other UN agencies have an impressive array of facilities designed to help. Where conflict

4. See Bibliography, page 123

arises between states in a region a UN Peacekeeping Force should be encouraged to act as barrier between them. This Force could also use its influence to promote reconciliation and conciliation until such time as the states themselves can find a permanent solution to their problems. If it became evident that the political will to resolve the region's differences was not forthcoming, those responsible for the UN Regional Peace and Development Fund could terminate funds to the development programme at any time during the five or ten year period.

If, however, a region found it difficult to reconcile its differences a non-official but well-known highly respected international Mediator could be asked to help. A proposal for such a group has been made by Professor Adam Curle called *In the Middle: Non Official Mediation in Violent Situations*.[5] Alternatively, official UN mediation should be sought.

4. Agreement to become a regional neutral and nuclear-free zone

Most, if not all, underdeveloped regions are seeking this objective. Unfortunately they are prevented from demanding this right by the domination of one or other of the Great Powers seeking spheres of influence in which to establish military bases in strategic areas around the world. Poor countries all too often are unable to preserve their independence because of being tied by economic necessity to one of these Great Powers. A peace and development programme would help the region to be economically independent and consequently feel free to establish itself as a neutral, nuclear-free zone.

The Great Powers may look at this part of the Code of Agreement with distaste, becuase it would hinder their world-wide power-seeking strategies; consequently they may refuse to help finance the proposed UN Peace and Development Fund; they may even attempt to sabotage the idea. Fortunately there are other sources of finance, namely, Britain and the other countries within the EEC, the Scandinavian countries, Canada, Australia, New Zealand, Japan, East and West Germany, Austria and the oil-rich nations. All these countries, especially those with large balance of payment surpluses such as Japan and the oil countries, should be promoting peaceful initiatives instead of leaving everything

5. See page 117

to the Great Powers. Financial support from these countries, especially in the early stages of development, would be preferable to reliance on the two major powers. Is it good for an international organization, especially the UN, to be financially dependent on one of the Great Powers? Instead these less powerful countries have the opportunity to play an important role in international affairs. Costa Rica, (one of the smallest and poorest of countries without an army) is showing what moral leadership can accomplish by encouraging the formation of the Central American Agreement, and a basic health service the envy of the Third World. This example of leadership could be emulated by other richer nations who alone have the funds to make visions a reality for 'where there is no vision the people perish'.

Later, assuming regional peace and development programmes were to be established and successful, even without Great Power participation, it is believed the USSR and the USA would then recognise the advantages of participating if only to avoid being made to appear uncaring and to prevent the leadership of the world passing to other hands. Sometimes the right thing is done for questionable motives. If this is so it is even possible we may then see the Great Powers vying with each other to capture the goodwill of world opinion; some believe this was the real reason which inspired the Marshall Plan.

If the promotion of regional peace, justice and human rights could be recognised as the primary aim of governments then Regional Peace and Development Programmes would be seen as a more realistic option than seeking spheres of influence and military bases which all too often fail in their objectives. The Great Powers will not change their policies easily or quickly, but this only strengthens the need for other nations to take the initiative as soon as possible, even if it is only in a small region, and then to proceed step by step, region by region, as success and the political will to succeed dictates.

5. *Agreement to institute Regional Conventions and a Regional Court of Human Rights analogous with the European Court of Human Rights*

This part of the Agreement is seen as an essential requirement for success because it would provide a safeguard for minorities against tyranny, and consequently make it more attractive for them to co-operate. It would also provide some assurance to a ruling party (such as the

White South Africans) that their social, economic and political human rights would be safeguarded. Only when safeguards against injustices, or the fear of injustices, are provided is it reasonable to expect those who strive for power, or those who have it, to co-operate for their mutual benefit.

Agreement to institute a Regional Court of Human Rights implies acceptance of the principle that each nation in the region will relinquish a small degree of national sovereignty to the Regional Court. It will also ensure that individuals who believe their freedoms are threatened by unlawful laws, or by the police exceeding their authority, can appeal to the Regional Court of Human Rights in a manner similar to that in which the European Court of Human Rights works in Europe. It is important that the rule of law applies equally to members of a government, the police and the judiciary if the abuse of power is to be avoided and good law enforced (this subject is dealt with at greater length in a later chapter).

Individual responsibility for 'crimes committed against peace, war crimes and crimes against humanity', as set out in the Nuremberg Principles and now widely accepted as recognised international law should be enforced at a regional level. This would mean setting up Regional Courts of Human Rights similar to that at Strasbourg and support for an International Criminal Tribunal.[6]

The threat to our freedoms today comes more and more frequently from within countries rather than from abroad. All governments, socialist and capitalist, love power and resent being under the law and all too often seek to impose their will on 'dissidents', 'terrorists', 'extremists' or 'freedom fighters', by denying freedom and justice to all. Thus instead of the law being seen as a safeguard to protect human rights it is frequently seen as an oppressive instrument of government bringing the police, the law, and the government into disrepute. The law must be seen to be just and in accordance with natural justice and the concept of natural law[7] or it will be flouted and seen to be the enemy of the people, thus exacerbating the very problem the law should be preventing. As more and more respect is gained for social, economic and political justice however, it is hoped the region itself would want to follow the example of Europe by including Regional Conventions and a

---

6. See pages 108–110
7. See the chapter 'The Nature of Law' on page 89

Regional Charter[8] so as to define clearly the nature of justice if all are to enjoy freedom under the law.

The Principles outlined above are considered to be the minimum requirement if the objectives of peace and development are to be reached but detailed negotiations will need to take place to define what is meant by 'development' as each region has very different circumstances and what may be suitable for one region may not be applicable for another. The Code of Agreement is seen as the means by which the greater objective of world peace may be attained and therefore it is hoped that as regions become stable and prosperous, based on social, economic and political justice, these ideals will be extended globally. The idea of international law, and its basis, are discussed in more detail in the chapters dealing with World Security and also The Future of the UN. The essential requirement, however, for the *implementation* of international law capable of preventing war effectively must be for the members of the UN to demand a UN International Criminal Tribunal before which individuals who commit war crimes and crimes against peace and humanity, as outlined in the Nuremberg Principles, can be arraigned. A UN Commissioner for Human Rights would also be needed to assemble evidence of crimes committed by individuals to be placed before the Tribunal. I believed that Regional Peace and Development Programmes would encourage this process by helping to create and nurture a favourable social, economic and political climate. These ideas have either been enacted by the UN or seriously proposed over a number of years by many respected authorities.[9]

It may be argued that the recipient nations will not be willing to accept 'conditionality' as proposed in the above Code of Agreement, but this objection has already been overcome by the example of the International Fund for Agricultural Development. It is suggested that the main criteria needed for the poor nations willingly to accept conditions must rest on a Code which is perceived to be fair and just and not in the short-term interest of the rich nations. They also need to have

---

8. See page 114
9. See pages 108−112

a decisive voice in the manner in which development programmes and peace-making ideas are implemented, otherwise trust and confidence will be absent and the basis of success destroyed. On the other hand the rich nations providing the funds want the assurance that their money will achieve the aims of peace, security, and development which rich and poor alike agree are today's priority. The Code of Agreement is therefore designed to provide the necessary means of co-operation between rich and poor.

Financing Regional Peace & Development Programmes

There have been many official reports, especially by the UN, about how to finance development programmes, and it is generally agreed that the obvious method would be to establish an effective relationship between disarmament and development; if only a fraction of the money spent on defence was redirected towards development, it is said the economic problems of the poor countries could be resolved with little difficulty.

Unfortunately the problem is not so simple. The leaders of the world are locked in an arms race and believe defence has a more important priority than development. How this priority can be reversed must be the long-term aim, while the immediate problem is to show how financing regional peace and development programmes is possible within the present financial restraints governments have imposed on themselves.

The long-term answer could be helped if we clarified our thinking on our objectives. We all probably agree that peace, freedom and security are desirable objectives, but differ in our thinking about how these ideals may be achieved. For instance, we can agree that a defence concept has many dangers; that there can be no defence against nuclear bombs; that nuclear war by accident is a real possibility; and that trust between nations is undermined by an arms race. Nevertheless, despite these dangers, governments continue to support war preparation because to do away with our defences would be to 'leave ourselves open to aggression' and therefore the 'deterrent' is better than 'being naked'. If, therefore, we seriously want to release for peaceful purposes the resources at present devoted to war preparation, it is essential for us to understand the nature of an alternative means of maintaining the peace based on enforceable international law. The Proposal for a regional approach shows how this can be brought about in a step-by-step manner. Once it is realized that we have an alternative to a defence concept costing, according to the Stockholm Peace Research Institute in 1980, 500 billion dollars a year in world terms or $110 per person on earth, there should be little difficulty in transferring a fraction of this sum to finance Regional Peace and Development Programmes as well as the existing UN agencies. This compares with official aid amounting to $29 billion. The problem is that we are psychologically brainwashed into believing in defence as the only means of maintaining our security and fail to consider realistically other better, perhaps cheaper alternatives. Nevertheless despite the constraints placed on us by a crippling defence programme it is possible to make a beginning now and the following are a few suggestions as to how this could be accomplished.

1. Working on the principle that a 'stitch in time saves nine' poverty could be overcome at a fraction of the money we now spend on 'aid'

For instance, large sums have been misused on inappropriate development such as nuclear power, large scale dams, cash crop mechanized growing of crops which could have been far better used on small scale grass-roots development programmes. The Third World is also spending (according to the Report *Disarmament and Development* by the Irish Commission for Justice and Peace in 1963) around eighty billion dollars, having doubled in the last ten years. Much of this money could be saved and re-directed into regional development. It is also generally recognised that poor administration in the Third World has often been the cause of large sums provided by the richer nations being misused, sums which could be saved by a Regional Secretariat supervising a regional development programme.

Good regional development programmes, initiated early, would encourage poor countries to co-operate and avoid conflict, the cause of most poverty. For instance, for a fraction of the money squandered on war or preparation for war in Ethiopia or Central America by the USA and the USSR, these regions could have achieved peace and prosperity. For instance, if the Quaker Ambulance Unit in Ethiopia, of which I was a member during the 1939−45 war, could have been given just one million pounds (not billion pounds) to promote rural development, planting trees and initiating small scale irrigation, appropriate education and medicine we may have been able to prevent the present famine. If this work could have been conducted within a regional concept the civil war could also have been avoided.

Small though the sums devoted to the Third World have been in the last forty or more years, (between 0.3 and 0.5% of Britain's Gross National Product) disappointing progress has been made and this has been largely due to the fact that development programmes have too often been irrelevant to the real needs of the people and have not been concerned to prevent the 120 wars in the Third World since 1945. We could obtain far better value for money by integrating social, economic and political regional programmes within a concept that is directly related to peace in the region.

2. *Development programmes should be linked with a disarmament programme based on regional security, releasing large sums from within the poor countries*

Defence spending in the Third World has increased proportionately even faster than in the Western World and is probably the major cause of poverty in poor countries. Our task is to help these countries to find peace with security so that their own resources can be released for constructive purposes. All too often the reverse has been the case in past years.

3. *Defence spending is a drain on the finances of the nations supplying the arms and should be redirected towards peaceful purposes*

Frequently military equipment is given as outright gifts, or at low rates of interest, supporting the 120 wars since 1945. Large sums have also been given, before war occurs, to many more countries in an attempt to maintain non-communist governments in power; this leads to a deterioration in social and economic conditions which in turn encourages revolt and the need for repressive measures. Sometimes this 'help' boomerangs as happened in the Falklands war when British-made guns were turned against British troops. In the Ethiopian war the USA and the USSR each gave military aid, first to one side, then the other. In doing so, Ethiopia's economy was almost destroyed, famine encouraged, and the need to help the country made many times more necessary than if aid had been given at a much earlier period. Clearly vast sums of money have been squandered supporting wars in the Third World on the assumption that it is all in the cause of peace only to see the situation in these regions become further destabilized and the situation made worse. If these vast sums of money had been used directly to help development programmes, the regions could have had peace and prosperity instead of famine, poverty and war. Costa Rica's example of turning guns into ploughshares and becoming an island of peace and prosperity in a region of war and poverty needs to be followed.

4. Another approach is the idea of 'parallelism'

By this is meant promoting regional peace and development programmes in one of the small regions of the world. These programmes could be initiated parallel with the government's present defence programmes and then, when development programmes proved successful, resources could be released to enable more ambitious regional development programmes to be initiated elsewhere. Gradually, region by region, the world would become a more peaceful place and disarmament become possible.

5. Funds given to the region would 'trigger off' the region's own resources

By giving the region the opportunity to put its 'house in order' and restore its economy, most of the funds needed for development could be generated within the region itself. Most regions of the world, if not all, could be self-sufficient and economically viable if they had peace and good administration. What keeps most countries in poverty is lack of co-operation at all levels, continual conflict and war and poor administration. Regional peace and development programmes would encourage co-operation, help with education, and seek an end to conflicts in the region. They would also insist on good administration and for the development programme to be appropriate to the real needs of the people. Resources spent by poor countries on expensive armaments could then be transferred to producing real wealth.

6. *Regional peace and development programmes could reconcile conflicts in the region*

There should be a permanent UN Peace and Development Fund in being many to which poor regions of the world could turn for help to resolve their difficulties. Countries in conflict should be encouraged to resolve their differences between themselves by helping them with adequate grants to co-operate. The Code of Agreement would require the countries to show they were making progress towards reconciling their differences by making full use of all the UN agencies, including a UN Peacekeeping Force. Compliance with the Code of Agreement would resolve the conflicts at less cost to the rich countries than engaging in military support for one side or the other. Outside 'solutions' are seldom satisfactory and every encouragement should be given for regions to resolve their own problems in their own way, provided this was done in accordance with justice and human rights.[1]

7. *The banking world urgently needs assurance that their money is safe in developing countries*

The present crisis, with several of the poor countries threatening to default on their debts, lends urgency to the problem. These debts are threatening to undermine the world's banking system, with possible disastrous results. Well-conceived regional peace and development programmes could remove this threat and bring about a sound financial economy within an agreed integrated regional plan, monitored by a Regional Secretariat. Commenting on Brazil's suspension of interest payments, the *Guardian* of February 24th 1987, says:

> what is needed to avoid this is nothing less than a new Marshall Plan.....a Marshall Plan would recognise that the reality of the matter is that some of the Third World's debts must be written down and rescheduled and that the financial supply lines from the industrialised countries must be re-opened.

---

1. See chapter 'Which Regions', page 54

8. *Multinational firms urgently need stable and prosperous regions in which to operate*

Regional peace and development programmes would give firms such as ICI and Unilever stable, favourable conditions thus encouraging them to invest in the region. These firms are frequently seen to be exploiting the poor countries by 'helping' with inappropriate aid, and this is not surprising if profit is the sole motive. If, however, they were encouraged to work within a clearly defined development programme which offered more opportunities for trade, they would probably welcome the change. Freedom for multinational firms in unstable conflict conditions is a poor alternative to helping the country to achieve real prosperity. Regional peace and development programmes could give them stable markets with a long-term future. Their expertise is urgently needed provided it is within a context such as an agreed development programme would provide. These firms need confidence if they are to invest in the future and earn valuable foreign exchange for the country in which they work. There is no reason why multinational firms should dictate terms once the nation state has economic independence assured under a regional development programme. Multinational firms have an important rôle to play in the poor world; if they had a clearly defined rôle and confidence in the future they could be valuable partners and consequently would probably invest more than they do.

9. *Proposals which have been before the UN include:*

a. In 1955 the French Prime Minister proposed the establishment of an International Fund for Development in which states would agree to reduce their military expenditures by a percentage each year, the resources to be transferred to the Fund.
b. In 1956 the Soviet Union proposed a similar special Fund. This proposal was repeated by the USSR as recently as 1987.
c. In 1964 Brazil proposed an Industrial Conversion and Economic Development Fund.
d. In 1973 the UN General Assembly supported a Soviet initiative calling for a 10 per cent reduction in military expenditure and 10 per cent of the funds saved to be for developing countries.
e. In 1978 Senegal proposed a similar tax.
f. At the tenth Special Session of the UN, France proposed an International Disarmament Fund.

g. Mexico supported the French initiative and proposed a special *ad-hoc* account in the UN Development Programme.

h. In 1978 Romania proposed the freezing and gradual reduction of military budgets by ten per cent with one half of the amounts to be transferred to the UN for development purposes.

The above are the barest outlines of some of the most important proposals put before the UN General Assembly and indicate the degree of international support for development programmes.

10. *Non-governmental initiatives*

The most notable non-governmental report in recent years has probably been the Brandt Report, *North, South, 1979*. This report calls for the establishment of a UN Regional Development Fund. The difference between the Brandt Proposal and the Proposal in this book is that the word 'Peace' is included in the name of the Fund; this addition makes a profound difference to the conception and administration of development programmes. Nevertheless similarities are close, each Proposal calling for substantial sums to be devoted to regional development.

The Report of the Socialist International Committee on Economic Policy, *Global Challenge, 1985*, chaired by Michael Manley, includes a promise to make 'a commitment to an additional spending of a hundred billion dollars a year to make possible a new decade of recovery and development'. Clearly if funds on this scale were forthcoming there would be little difficulty promoting Regional Peace and Development Programmes.

11. *Peace Tax campaign*

In several countries there are campaigns for a Peace Tax. These campaigns aim to persuade governments to introduce legislation so that individuals who object to paying for war or military preparation on the grounds of conscience, or conviction, may legally have their contribution redirected to uses morally acceptable. If this legislation was introduced the democratic process would discover the extent of support for overseas development. Introduced globally, an internationally organized Peace Tax may even succeed in surpassing the hundred billion dollars committed by the Socialist International Committee.

Governments are frequently well behind the people in demonstrating their goodwill, as the Bob Geldof appeal to relieve the Ethiopian famine demonstrated.

13. Co-operating with the Commonwealth or the EEC

Both these organizations have expressed their interest in promoting regional development programmes. The Commonwealth with its world-wide commitments and common sense of purpose and understanding could be an ideal organization to promote a Commonwealth Peace and Development Programme. The EEC is in a similar situation and has the added advantage that it already has at its disposal large sums of Community money to be used for development work through the Lomé agreement. [2]

14. Recycling of International Funds

The financial crisis facing the world caused by the lack of confidence in the USA economic situation threatens all the Western world with the possibility of a world slump.

To compound the problem the Third World's debts are accumulating at a rate which threatens to make repayment impossible.

Both these issues are threatening to undermine, not only the financial institutions such as the banks and Wall Street, but the social, economic fabric of all societies around the world thus creating the ideal breeding ground for poverty, social unrest, extremist governments, conflict and war.

Clearly the situation demands urgent action and the most practical one which could resolve both problems would be to inject investment into the Third World by redirecting funds from defence spending to promoting real peace through supporting the proposed UN Peace and Development Fund and Regional Peace and Development Programmes.

Alternatively those nations which received most aid from the Marshall Plan, particularly West Germany and Japan, who now have favourable balances of payments, should be encouraged to provide the funds. Seldom have moral and selfish interests been so

---

2. See page 108

identical. If something is not done then all may suffer; on the other hand the sacrifice of 1% or 2% of their GNP to finance a UN Peace and Development Fund would restore financial confidence around the world, promote world trade and create favourable conditions for a healthy world order free from the fear of war. All countries would benefit and the threat of a world economic slump be averted.

15. Appreciation of a New Era

The period since about the 1980s has been marked by a slow but important and largely unnoticed change in the attitudes of the nations of the world, particularly the Great Powers. It seems the nations of the world have been learning the hard way that seeking spheres of influence, or power bases around the world by military means is futile and often counter-productive. The wars in Vietnam, Ethiopia and Afghanistan, for instance, have been very expensive and unrewarding and there is now great reluctance and much more caution by all nations to become involved in any war no matter how small. The USA and the USSR also seem to be realizing the enormous cost of the arms race and are seeking ways of reducing the burden. The USSR has even suggested (in August 1987) using some of the money saved from disarmament for development programmes. The climate of opinion is slowly changing and there is now a great opportunity for those of us who want peaceful solutions to encourage co-operation for our survival in regions where vital interests are involved. Regional Peace and Development Programmes could, for instance, be encouraged simultaneously in regions such as Latin America and South East Asia.[3]

16. Enlightened self interest reasons

John Donne's Devotions sums up the problem in his meditation when he says, 'No man is an island... and any man's death diminishes me'. This well-known saying is more true today than ever before. Thanks to modern communications, the world is now one large village, and what hurts a part hurts the whole. For example the Marshall Plan was initiated because to have allowed Europe to collapse would also have affected the USA. Moral and economic reasons therefore demanded urgent action. The example of the Marshall Plan needs to

---

3. See chapter 'Which Regions?' on page 54

be emulated. We cannot sit back and watch the poor world remain in poverty, with some of the countries being in desperate poverty, when we have it in our power to restore their economies. Today, more than ever before in mankind's history we are dependent on each other for our survival. Self-interest with a moral concern for the well-being of others is therefore today's most pressing need. The two can be made compatible through Regional Peace and Development Programmes.

The Future of the UN

During the past decade several important Reports have been written, each offering solutions for reforming the UN. In 1969 we had the Jackson Report, and in 1975 the Dag Hammarskjold Report; both have been quietly buried. More recently, to mark the occasion of the 40th anniversary of the UN, a Study called *The Future of the UN System* was made by the International Foundation for Development Initiatives. Several unofficial Reports have also been made, most notably the Brandt Report.

All these Reports made excellent recommendations but, valuable though they are, it is doubtful if they will be accepted in the near future because they require major changes in the constitution and organization of the UN which are unacceptable to the member states, especially when it is necessary to obtain ratification between two thirds of the member states including the five permanent members of the Security Council each with very different perceptions of what is required.

The change which the Proposal for Regional Peace and Development Programmes suggest could be implemented without difficulty would need only a few of the richer nations of the world (not necessarily including the USA) to support the idea. Regional solutions would also be much easier to initiate and implement than global solutions. The idea of regional solutions could grow naturally region by region ultimately to involve most of the world, with each one becoming a region of peace with effective law supporting human rights. These regions should each owe their loyalty to the UN for economic and political reasons. A regional approach would also integrate many of the existing institutions of the UN and thereby avoid the present overlapping and undue bureaucracy endemic in the UN. Eventually the influence of successful regions of peace and development, each owing its success to the UN, would generate a new climate of opinion in the world favourable to supporting the UN. Thus reform of the UN could be accomplished in a pragmatic manner based on natural growth without disrupting the existing constitution of the UN with all the delay and problems such an attempt would entail.

Gradually, as more and more regions become regions of peace and development, and respect for social, economic, and political human rights are extended around the world, a new philosophy regarding the role of the UN would be nurtured. This belief is supported by socio-logical evidence that when environmental conditions change, people's reactions to that environment change. Slowly, as conditions within the regions improved, nationalistic attitudes would be transformed into regional loyalties as has been demonstrated by the example of Europe in recent years. Respect for human rights could also be reinforced by regional courts of law, to give protection to the peoples in the region from injustice which may be imposed by their own governments.

This change in perception of the rule of law in the regions could subsequently be extended to reform the UN. Individual responsibility under the rule of law should become universally accepted as the alternative to the idea of 'collective security', an idea unfortunately still cherished by many influential leaders of public opinion as the fundamental basis of the UN's authority. The concept of 'collective security' was conceived as the means of enforcing international law but in reality it has been responsible for the failure of the League of Nations and the loss of confidence in the UN.

The reasoning for this failure has been brilliantly argued by Mrs H.M. Swanwick in her book *Collective Insecurity*[1] in which she declares bluntly that sanctions between sovereign states can never work; on the contrary they increase our insecurity by reliance on fear. The theory that if a nation infringed the sovereignty of another, especially by military means, the combined weight of all the other nations of the world would prevent it has the ring of common sense, but in reality it is impractical, being based on a false premise. Experience has shown that, in practice, the idea of collective security increases suspicions, fear and divisions when trust, confidence and co-operation are most needed. In short, its own philosophy undermines the basis of

1. See the chapter 'A Search for World Order' by Dr. Avery Joyce in *Foundations of Peace and Freedom*

its authority. A different philosophy based on nurturing a new social, economic and political environment could rejuvenate the regions and subsequently the UN by giving them a new meaning and purpose.

The false philosophy of collective security was clearly exposed by the Italian-Abyssinian war in the 1930s and the Korean War in the 1950s. In both instances the concept of collective security, which should so easily, in theory, have prevented war, led instead to the Ethiopian war, which in turn led to the League of Nations falling into disrepute and as a consequence encouraged the German and Italian dictators to expand their territories and led directly to the Second World War.

The Korean War almost led the UN into a Third World War against North Korea. What started as a UN enforcement operation under Article 42 resulted in the USA, and a few of her allies, waging war against a Korean army supported by the USSR and China. Since then there has been a de-facto recognition by most nations that the philosophy of 'collective security' is an illusion, and no further military actions have been attempted by the UN. Nevertheless the illusion still continues to be held, that the ideal is collective security.

These past failures have proved Mrs. Swanwick's thesis that attempts to implement the idea of 'collective security' are a sure recipe for collective *insecurity*. Even the limited attempts to impose the will of the UN by the use of economic sanctions has proved ineffectual and sometimes counter-productive. The idea that international law can be enforced by the use of violence, or coercion, is sadly mistaken and must therefore be discarded in exchange for international law based on very different foundations. For the UN to pass resolutions condemning violations of the UN Charter and then to see those resolutions ignored with impunity has undermined confidence in the UN's authority.

Unfortunately, although the failures of the League of Nations in Ethiopia and the UN in Korea have demonstrated the impracticality of collective security,[2] the alternative is not clearly perceived and consequently the UN is often regarded as an organization which has no real sense of mission for today's world. Having abandoned one philosophy it has not yet learnt a new one. Peace, like health, cannot be commanded instantly, but will only be achieved by encouraging and nurturing many factors, all of which need to be integrated into

---

2. Discussed in chapter on 'World Security', page 73

a structure, and organization such as the Proposal for Regional Peace and Development seeks to promote.

Fortunately good progress has been made by UN agencies such as UNESCO, UNDP, UNICEF, UNRWA, WHO and the UN Development Programme despite the criticisms and lack of support from many countries. The UN has now accumulated a wealth of knowledge, experience, and expertise upon which we can build. What is needed, therefore, is the political will and a new philosophy to encourage a new UN agency dedicated to promoting peaceful relationships, such as this Proposal suggests whereby this knowledge, experience and expertise can be co-ordinated and implemented by a qualified Secretariat based in the region.

The failures of many development programmes have often been caused by the inability of the UN to integrate political issues within economic solutions. Usually political and economic issues are considered in separate compartments by the UN, yet clearly if poverty in the poor regions of the world is to be abolished, and conflicts in the regions resolved, the two approaches must be undertaken within a structure of co-operation.

Progress in this direction would mean a changed social and economic environment removing many injustices and encouraging a changed climate of opinion in support of regional law. Regional solutions would also be much easier, fairer, and more efficient to administer than the limited role employed by the IMF, or the World Bank. These organizations are constrained to limit their aid to that of rescuing the financial fortunes of a country or region. Their constitution also makes them dependent on the financial institutions of the West and this limits their ability to provide the kind of aid best suited for a developing country. It also means that political considerations often determine the manner in which development programmes are considered and such aid is usually given in loan form, increasing the debts of poor countries and consequently making them even more vulnerable to unrest and greater poverty. Most loans given by the IMF and the World Bank in the past have been given to single countries, but recent changes point in the direction of regional concepts. The proposal for a UN Peace and Development Fund on the other hand is designed to perform a much more radical improvement by injecting increased aid in grant form and on a scale adequate to ensure the region's full recovery. The constitution and personnel involved administering the Fund should also be carefully considered to ensure their independence and the trust and confidence of all concerned.

The beauty of this proposal is that it could be initiated quickly, needing only enough funds from a few of the richer nations immediately to enable a UN Peace and Development Fund to promote the first Regional Peace and Development Programme. Long drawn out consultations lasting years with no assurance of success could be avoided. Success in one region it is hoped would encourage all the other nations in the world to support the idea of regional development with a financial commitment so that more and more regions could be helped.

One of the main criticisms levelled against the UN is that it is riddled with bureaucracy and its overhead costs are excessive. Regional Peace and Development Programmes would overcome this problem by requiring a qualified Secretariat to supervise the regional programme. The manner in which the Marshall Plan was administered demonstrated that a small Secretariat composed of experienced individuals with proven ability could efficiently encourage and monitor a large regional development programme controlled by the countries involved, in accordance with an agreed programme. A Regional Peace and Development Programme, asked for a region, and funded by a UN Regional Peace and Development Fund would co-ordinate all activities in the region and reduce its overhead costs.

Another advantage would be that many of the conflict situations in the world, such as those in Southern Africa, Southern America or South East Asia, could be resolved peacefully if there was in being a UN Peace and Development Fund which regions could turn to for help.[3] The potentialities for reconciliation and conciliation through Regional Peace and Development programmes must be seen to be one of its most important functions. Development, reconciliation and the promotion of human rights should therefore all be devolved to the regional level where co-operation between the proposed regional Secretariat and the UN Peace and Development Fund could be exercised with the minimum of difficulty and maximum efficiency.

It is also widely believed that the UN suffers from an administration dominated by politics and a top-heavy administration absorbing too large a proportion of development funds, thus making it difficult for UN

---

3. See chapter 'Which Regions?'

agencies to maintain their independence. To overcome these problems the proposed UN Peace and Development Fund should be founded on principles which insisted that all personnel involved at regional and international level were chosen for their personal qualities and who owed their first allegiance to the UN. A fair representation of members should also be recruited from the Third World subject only to their personal abilities. To ensure trust and confidence between the members of the UN Peace and Development Fund and the members of the region, development programmes should be administered by a Secretariat whose members would be drawn from outside politics. Suitable individuals may be found in the various UN agencies, in the many charities working in the Third World, or from the universities. The criteria for appointment must rest solely on their expertise and on their ability to win the trust and confidence of all concerned.

A promising region of Regional Peace and Development Programmes could be the Caribbean. Canada and Britain are already contributing large sums to this region. The Commonwealth also came out strongly in favour of regional development programmes in the Report of the Commonwealth Consultative Group under the title of *Vulnerability - Small States in a Global Society*, presented to the Commonwealth Conference in Nassau in 1985.[4] If, therefore, difficulties are encountered in promoting a UN Peace and Development Fund, it is proposed that the Commonwealth should initiate the idea. In many ways it would be easier to undertake the task under Commonwealth auspices because there is already a degree of trust and confidence between its members, virtues essential for a successful conclusion. There is also a strong tradition of regional co-operation in the Caribbean, and as all the states involved are members of the Commonwealth, agreement between them should be easier to find than in some other regions. The important need is for an early initiative to set the idea in motion. Once it is seen to be achieving its objectives it is hoped the idea would soon be copied and incorporated into the UN.

The Pacific Islands are another region where a Regional Peace and Development Programme, is needed. Australia and New Zealand are both anxious to promote regional initiatives for peace in this area and have expressed interest in regional development. If Japan, with its large financial reserves, were to help, these three countries could no doubt

4. See page 107

promote a Pacific Regional Peace and Development Programme. Japan does not seem fully to appreciate its potential for promoting the peace of the world. The huge favourable balance of payments Japan holds, which threatens the economic stability of the Western world, could be used instead to finance the proposed UN Peace and Development Fund. Similar arguments could be used for Saudi Arabia and Western Germany. These three countries by themselves could change the face of world politics and lay the foundations for a revitalised UN providing it with new authority and respect.

'Trade not aid' not long ago was the catch-phrase for the developing world; today the slogan is 'aid is not enough'. Unfortunately both slogans are inadequate. Trade can be positively harmful when it encourages inappropriate development, and although aid is not enough in itself, it is still desperately needed. The idea behind both concepts is well intentioned, but both fail to come to grips with the primary cause of poverty which is conflict and war and the preparations for war and all the consequent waste of resources. What is therefore wanted by most poor countries is to become more self-sufficient to avoid having to compete for world markets to pay for imports they need but cannot afford. Poor nations could be encouraged to become more self-sufficient and more self-reliant within a regional context with each region co-operating on a global scale. This principle is an idea which could be encouraged by all the nations of the world to help each of them to regain control of their own destiny. We need the utmost co-operation between nations but each nation also needs economic freedom within an agreed international structure if it is to express its own identity and dignity within the community of nations. How to harmonize unity with diversity at all levels is perhaps the main problem facing mankind today and Regional Peace and Development Programmes are seen as the answer.

Poor countries need aid, but if war continues to plague a country it is almost a waste of resources. Regional Peace and Development Programmes would avoid this problem by concentrating on appropriate development but within a framework which encourages regional co-operation and peaceful relationships. This is why emphasis is placed on an integrated programme within a regional context. To achieve this aim a Code of Agreement would be

---

5. See chapter 'Code of Agreement', page 19

needed between the proposed UN Peace and Development Fund and a region.[5]

Development programmes, as at present conceived, valuable though they are, have too limited a vision; their horizons should be extended to include bringing peace to the region. The problem therefore is to understand how, and why, development programmes can help to promote effective international law. This problem is discussed in other chapters and finds the answer lies in supporting the concept of Natural Law in the belief that, if the *basis* of international law is clearly perceived, the effective means of maintaining peace becomes within our grasp. If respect for law within the regions and co-operation with the many UN agencies could be encouraged by regional programmes it is reasonable to believe respect for international law would be gradually extended to the UN itself.

For such law to be effective, however, demands adequate machinery for enforcing it. Proposals for an International Criminal Tribunal and for an International Commissioner for Human Rights have been before the UN for a long time. If these institutions could be established, free from political interference, the alternative to collective security as a means of ensuring our peace and freedoms would be assured.

International law has already been formulated, in the Nuremberg Principles, but because there are no courts of law to adjudicate and enforce them they remain a faint shadow of their potential. However even without the sanction of international courts they provide a valuable yardstick by which to judge individual behaviour of past government leaders, as in Argentina. If these Principles, however, were to have the full support of governments, and international courts were established, war could be outlawed. Wars, it must be remembered, are first promoted by individual politicians in governments and implemented by individual soldiers; therefore it is only by making individuals responsible for their actions before an international court that international law can be enforced. It is also easier to bring an individual to a court of law once the necessary international courts of law are in being than to act against a nation which refuses to accept the verdict of the Security Council. Law can be enforced against an individual without a serious risk of war, it cannot be enforced against a nation determined to 'commit a crime against peace', or 'against humanity', as declared in the Nuremberg Principles.

The advantage of the above process for enforcing international law is that it can be promoted regionally whenever there is the request for a development programme, with each region knowing in advance what is involved. When these become regions of peace and neutrality, the rule of law based on human rights and economic well-being would be established.

By placing the emphasis on the rule of law within a region, based on the concept of Natural Law,[6] a gradual change of emphasis within the UN would occur, as has happened in the Council of Europe. The rule of law within Europe has grown naturally as a consequence of co-operation and respect for human rights; the same could happen on a global scale providing similar fertile conditions prevailed. Regional Peace and Development Programmes would seek to create these conditions, region by region. The progress that has been made towards limiting national sovereignty in Europe is remarkable, with 21 states voluntarily surrendering an important element of sovereignty to a European Court of Human Rights. No element of violence has been used to create this situation, if it had been it would have destroyed all trust and confidence between members of the Council of Europe and consequently all respect for regional law.

The reform of the UN could come about gradually in a similar manner to that which has happened in Europe, as trust and confidence between nations increases *within* and *between* the regions, based on the same principles which have encouraged trust and confidence between the nations of Europe. At present disputes between nations are taken to the Security Council for political settlement, when frequently a settlement according to the rule of law as it affects individuals is more appropriate. Seldom, if ever, have attempts to coerce a nation led to a satisfactory conclusion. I therefore suggest that many of the disputes could be resolved more effectively by a Commissioner for Human Rights assembling evidence of violations of human rights, committed by individuals, and taking this evidence before the International Criminal Tribunal; a judgement about the individual responsible could then be made. In some instances the threat or possibility of world publicity alone will be sufficient to deter an individual committing a crime, but if the publicity proved inadequate there are many non-violent sanctions which could be applied, such as making the individual

6. As outlined in the chapter dealing with Natural Law, page 89

persona non grata around the world, being unable to find asylum and having his assets taken from him. If it is difficult to prove the guilt of an individual ordering a crime it should be easier to identify the offender because crimes are committed by junior officials, or army personnel. Implementing international law at this level should therefore be possible once the necessary agreements and machinery for its enforcement have been found. The principle works within nations and within federal states; there is therefore no reason to believe it should not work on an international level given a favourable social and economic environment which Regional Peace and Development Programmes seek to promote.

Individuals in all regions should also be entitled to assert their human rights in a court of law. This is already European law and is a valuable protection against nation states infringing human rights. European law has been formulated into a Convention declaring that the fundamental freedoms of justice and peace are best maintained by an effective political democracy and a common understanding and observance of human rights. Today all 21 members of the council of Europe have ratified the European Convention of Human Rights; this Convention recognises that individuals have certain rights and that where an individual claims there has been a violation of his rights he can initiate proceedings for redress against the government he holds responsible. The Convention is a form of contract under which states accept certain duties. Since the Convention was formulated, new rights and obligations have been added in what are known as Protocols. States can choose which Protocols to accept and many have been widely adopted. This example of Europe illustrates the way international law may be freely accepted by independent regions. Governments are obliged to see that those within their jurisdiction have their human rights and freedoms protected under the Convention or under one of the Protocols. Failure to comply may lead to any one of the member states in the Council of Europe who have ratified the Convention or Protocols, finding itself being taken by an individual to the European Court of Human Rights whose verdict is final. This is a revolutionary change in the progress of mankind which could have a profound influence on the manner law is administered in the future.

The example and influence of Europe has been felt around the world, because it is the first regional attempt to give the individual the right to be protected by law from oppression, or the denial of his human rights, by his own government. This protection is a valuable way of reducing, and often removing, the causes of conflict.

It seems that most recognised authorities versed in law around the world want to emulate the Council of Europe's example, but because their governments frequently feel they must retain the freedom to interpret the law in their own way, for economic reasons, or to maintain their power, these good intentions (even when formulated into solemn agreements such as the African Charter) remain unenforceable. Regional Peace and Development Programmes however would give the regions the social, economic and political security needed to enable Regional Conventions to become a reality, and the incentive for the people in the region to insist on something being done to make them effective.

The above process of nurturing good international law needs extending to the UN. Instead of the Security Council trying to impose its will on a nation, the rule of law would operate under the law, not by the dictates of political manoeverings in political gatherings which frequently generate more heat than light. Most nations do not wish to appear before the world as uncivilized, and will fall over backwards to give the appearance of upholding human rights. This process could be further encouraged by the politicians concerned knowing they may be taken before a World Court of Human Rights if they personally violated agreed Conventions. Even today, without a World Court, modern communications in radio, TV, and transport, make politicians far more sensitive to world opinion than would otherwise be the case. Politicians are very jealous of their image and go to great lengths to protect it. This influence of public opinion could be further extended if members of the UN agreed to encourage UNESCO to assemble more information and news of events, and distribute it through a Regional UN radio, TV and news service. Such a service could, over a period of time earn the UN a reputation for accurate and reliable news and information, thus preventing news and information being manipulated for propaganda purposes. This is already happening in small ways but is discouraged by governments who do not understand its relevance to world peace. Regional Peace and Development Programmes could encourage governments in the regions to appreciate that their security depends upon their support for international law based on the respect for human rights, and that respect for human rights depends largely on access to good information.

A great step forward in the right direction was taken on June 26th 1987 when the UN Convention Against Torture came into force. 'It will now be possible to try people guilty of acts of torture in any state which is a party to the convention, if they are not extradited' (*Forum* October 1987). By an amazing coincidence, June 26 1987 also marked the coming into force of the European Convention for the prevention of torture and inhuman or degrading treatment or punishment. (*Forum* October 1987). Unfortunately the international control machinery is still weak; for example only six of the first twenty states ratifying the Convention have agreed to allow the committee to examine complaints by individuals or other states. Nevertheless the rule of law enforceable by non-violent means is now a fact. Every effort should be made, especially by the peace movement, to strengthen this process by encouraging all governments to ratify the Convention without reservations. Regional Peace and Development Programmes would support this process by encouraging a favourable social, economic and political climate of opinion.

Law also requires that justice is even-handed and applied to all who violate human rights whether the individual involved is a member of the public, the police, or the government. Only by making individuals responsible for their own actions can the waging of war itself be made difficult and even impossible. 'War will stop when men refuse to fight' has long been a slogan in the peace movement; if this Proposal were implemented it could become a reality and international law become effective enough to arraign individuals before an International Criminal Tribunal. Individuals would then be loth to commit crimes on the order of a superior officer, or the officer on the orders of a head of government. Thus all soldiers would at least hesitate before committing crimes as defined by the Nuremberg Principles, such as 'crimes against peace' or 'humanity'. If we can achieve this level of international law war itself would be outlawed because the first requirement of a soldier is obedience to a command, right or wrong. If the soldier has a higher duty to question a command, and the right to refuse under international law, then waging war becomes almost impossible. The Nuremberg Principles, which are already recognised as having the force of international law, would be given real authority, and the peace we seek would be within our grasp reinforced by an International Criminal Tribunal.

The principle is universally recognised today as international law and is even being actively pursued in countries such as Argentina where those generals who committed crimes against humanity a few years ago, are being court-marshalled. Lieutenant Calley, who committed crimes against humanity in Vietnam was also court-marshalled and found guilty under the Nuremberg Principles; American, British and German army manuals also declare that a soldier is only obliged to obey lawful orders, which, under international law includes the Nuremberg Principles.[7]

In view of the progress already made towards the rule of law in Europe and in the UN, as outlined above, the concept of maintaining world peace under the rule of law is not as outlandish as it may at first appear. In fact peace under the law is within our grasp if only we could find the political will to institute the social and economic basis of international law founded on the Declaration of Human Rights. Considering the danger we are in, the reality is that there is no alternative and a further step in this direction could be taken tomorrow.

This chapter has considered the long-term vision and while it is appreciated that this vision cannot be implemented immediately, I believe that it is well within our capacity to initiate a development programme in one of the regions in the very near future and then to proceed step by step, region by region to improve and modify it.

It is sometimes said there is little wrong with the UN which its members could not remedy by giving it more support, and there is much truth in this assertion. The problem is that this support is not being given, and is not likely in the immediate future on the scale needed unless there is a radical change in people's attitudes. This is not surprising considering the difficulties involved in uniting 150 nations each with very different problems and conflicting interests. The answer is to encourage the UN to resolve its problems in those regions where national interests could be overcome in a pragmatic manner suitable for that particular region. Global solutions, such as agreements on maritime law and the promotion of international courts of law must still of course remain the responsibility of the UN, but the main thrust of its work should be to encourage the establishment of regions of peace and prosperity within an economic framework that supports global solutions. The UN needs to resemble a world co-operative with each member recognising its responsibilities

7. See pages 108, 109 and 112

to the co-operative for the sake of its own survival. By encouraging the decentralisation of power within the region to its smallest units, such as the Cantons in Switzerland, within a structure which integrates social, economic and political human rights but with each unit owing its first allegiance to the UN, the UN could be rejuvenated and become similar to a co-operative organization in which all members owe their loyalty for their own good and for the good of all. Global solutions would then be possible.

Which Regions?

Many poor regions of the world are striving to become Regional Communities encouraged by the example of the European Economic Community, but for many reasons are unable to do so. If, however, there was the opportunity for them to ask for economic aid, similar to that under the Marshall Plan which enabled Western Europe to co-operate and recover from the devastation of war, there is little doubt that many of them would request assistance, provided the conditions were seen to be fair and in accordance with their natural aspirations of freedom and justice.

The reasons preventing these regions from co-operating are many but most poor countries have large debt problems which have made them forfeit some of their independence either to one of the Great Powers or to one or more of the multinational companies. Their debts also force them to encourage cash exports which in turn distorts their economies making them dependent on fluctuating world prices to the detriment of local self-sufficiency. In addition, the Great Powers are always seeking spheres of influence, either for economic gain or to obtain a military presence; this often takes away a further degree of national independence and causes resentment. Generous regional economic aid would remove these difficulties.

The advantage of obtaining financial help on a regional basis (in contrast to nations receiving aid individually) is that it would give all the nations in the region the incentive to co-operate. Above all, it would help them resolve their conflicts and become regions of peace.

The world community, who provide the funds, should be motivated by enlightened self-interest reasons in the knowledge that this is one world and that to allow a part to remain in poverty or participate in war is to harm the whole. This attitude was well described by General

54

Marshall when he outlined the principles which inspired the Marshall Plan by saying:

> It is logical that the United States should do whatever it is able to do to assist the return to normal economic health of the world. Our policy is not against any country or doctrine but against hunger, poverty, desperation and chaos. Its purpose should be the revival of a working economy in the world so as to permit the emergence of political and social conditions in which free institutions can exist.[1]

This objective of Marshall's 'to assist the return to normal economic health of the world' should also be our objective. We now have many advantages compared to the days of 1947 when Marshall announced his Plan. The rich world today is vastly richer; we have had 40 years' post-war experience working in development programmes and perhaps most important of all we have been able to learn from the European experience. Consequently we are now in a far better position to initiate similar regional programmes than in 1947.

The questions may be asked, what do you mean by a region? and, where do you suggest we start?

To the first of these questions there can be no clear cut answer. Regions can be as large as a continent, or as small as an island. A very small region may therefore be part of a much larger region but this fact should not prevent it from applying for help. A large region would only have difficulty in receiving help because it would probably need more financial help than may be available.

To make a region eligible for help it should have two problems to resolve. First, the need to overcome its internal conflicts; secondly, its need for a development programme to overcome poverty. A third requirement would be that all the parties involved should make a joint approach for help knowing in advance the nature of agreement needed before help is given.

To the second question, where should a start be made?, there is again no clear-cut answer. All would depend on the region itself making an application to the proposed UN Peace and Development Fund. There should be no question of coercing a region but all regions would know of the availability of a peace and development programme and the nature of the proposed Code of Agreement necessary to obtain

---

1. See page 102

that help. If this help is adequate to achieve its declared purpose of achieving peace and development on a scale similar to the Marshall Plan, and the Code of Agreement is in accordance with the region's own aspirations for social, economic and political human rights, there would be no shortage of regions requesting assistance. The regions suggested are those thought to be most suitable but they should by no means be considered to be the best or only regions suitable.

A Code of Agreement is necessary because, before aid is given, especially if in grant form, there must be some assurance that the aims of peace and economic development will be achieved, not only to satisfy the nations giving the financial help, but also to assure the recipients of help that their legitimate social and economic needs will be met. Some regions may feel that the conditions suggested in the Code of Agreement[2] may infringe their national sovereignty, but the belief is held that if the conditions necessary are in accordance with the natural aspirations of the people involved they will appreciate the disciplines necessary, especially if the details can be negotiated.

It will probably be said that some of the governments in the regions discussed below will never agree to accept the conditions requested in the Code of Agreement, and there may be some truth in this criticism. What is overlooked however, is the tremendous longing of all peoples everywhere for social, economic and political justice. Once this longing is harnessed, even the most ruthless of governments cannot prevent a change. For example, in recent years we have witnessed several such changes; in Argentina, in Uganda, in the Philippines, and in Iran. These changes occurred in countries with ruthless dictatorships and indicate that even the most tyrannical government is not immune to change once the popular will for social change is overwhelming.

The belief is held that if the United Nations encouraged these social forces for change, governments would have to reflect the popular will or be rejected. The principle involved would not be very different from that of states wishing to join the Council of Europe. In Europe those states outside the Council of Europe who wish to join know in advance the disciplines of democracy which must be observed if their application is to be considered. This advance knowledge by the public and governments in the country needing help, increases the internal pressures for constructive change, encourages co-operation between

---

2. See page 19 *et seq.*

antagonistic groups, and puts pressure on governments to observe human rights.

If the funds raised for a UN Peace and Development Fund were insufficient to initiate a large Regional Peace and Development Fund, only a small region could be helped in the first instance. Later, when regional development programmes were proved to be successful, more funds, it is hoped, would be forthcoming, thus enabling more Regional Peace and Development Programmes to be supported around the world.

It may sometimes be found that a region in desperate need has within its borders a community with a high standard of living, (eg the Whites in South Africa within the Southern African region); it may then be asked why should they also benefit when they have no need? The answer is that by defining, and agreeing, about what is meant by development, in the Code of Agreement, help would be directed specifically to improving the standard of living for the poorest in the region as a whole even if one part of the region is very rich. Although the Whites in South Africa for instance would no doubt indirectly benefit from a Regional Peace and Development Programme, the help from the Peace and Development Fund would be given essentially to promote the social, economic and political well-being of the poor in all the states in the region.

THE EAST CARIBBEAN ISLANDS

The Caribbean consists of many scattered islands each jealous of its own identity but each urgently needing to co-operate with the others. This need to co-operate has been widely recognised in the past and several serious attempts have been made to create a Federation. In the early 1960s there was hope of forming a West Indian Federation following the British, American, Dutch and French withdrawal from the area, and the idea has continued to be on the agenda ever since.

Canada, Britain and Trinidad (an oil-producing island in the Caribbean) are already providing funds for the Caribbean countries, while the EEC is helping and is planning further investment on a regional basis [3]

Further help may be available from the Commonwealth in view of the decisions reached at the last Commonwealth Conference

---

3. See page 108

held in Nassau in 1985, (which included several Caribbean heads of state). This Conference approved a Report of its Consultative Group[4] encouraging regional initiatives especially for small states such as those in the Caribbean. The Conference's final Communiqué 'endorsed the Report's emphasis on the increased potential for action at the regional level'. There is therefore no lack of support for a regional initiative; what is now needed is for help to be channelled through an organization structured to integrate social, economic and political issues, and adequate to put the region on a sound long-term economic basis, as suggested in this Proposal.

Ideally all efforts to encourage regional programmes should be through the proposed UN Peace and Development Fund, but there is no reason why this should prevent the Commonwealth or the EEC from taking the initiative, especially as both these organizations already have close associations with the region and are providing considerable sums for development. Either, or both, these organizations could initiate a Commonwealth or EEC Peace and Development Fund for the Caribbean.

SOUTH-EAST ASIA

This war-torn, tragic region, comprising Vietnam, Kampuchea, Laos and Thailand should form a natural region. Before the war in Vietnam, the UN financed a very imaginative development programme based on the Mekong River. This river runs through Kampuchea with its tributaries in Laos and Thailand; consequently a development programme based on this river could help to unite all these countries in peaceful endeavour. The Mekong River Project should be recommenced within a regional development programme which includes Vietnam.

It is known that Vietnam is anxious to withdraw from Kampuchea but she fears that if she does so Pol Pot, or his followers, will return and again threaten Vietnam's security. A Regional Peace and Development Programme implemented over several years would encourage the restoration of economic, social and political human rights and consequently promote prosperity and independence with a Regional Court of Human Rights. Within such a framework the fear of an unfriendly

---

4. See page 107

Kampuchean government would be diminished. Only when that fear is reduced may we expect Vietnam freely to leave Kampuchea. She may hesitate to leave during the first year of participating in a regional development programme but the Code of Agreement could stipulate a time-table for her withdrawal. This withdrawal would be made easier by all the states in the region agreeing to the Code of Agreement.

The countries of Laos, Kampuchea, and Vietnam suffered more bombs than were used in all the Second World War yet their 'crime' was to fight for their freedom against foreign oppression. The war in Vietnam overflowed into Kampuchea and Laos and infected Thailand which now accommodates thousands of refugees on its borders, many of whom support the dreaded Pol Pot regime, now a continual threat to the security of Kampuchea. If ever a region deserved the world's compassion it is South East Asia.

It is often said in the Western world that until Vietnam withdraws from Kampuchea no aid can be given: but Vietnam cannot withdraw until it is assured that a friendly, or at least non-aggressive government will rule in Kampuchea. Unfortunately, until this assurance is found the Vietnamese will remain despite the fact that keeping their troops in Kampuchea is a severe drain on their own depleted resources. A Regional Peace and Development Programme could provide the conditions for a friendly government to be installed thus enabling the Vietnamese troops to be withdrawn.

The solution to all these problems lies primarily with Thailand who encourage and support anti-Vietnamese forces on her borders with Kampuchea. This encouragement is self-defeating because it only results in strengthening the resolve of the Vietnamese to remain in Kampuchea in order to maintain a government in power which is not hostile to her.

The answer to this long-standing problem is to urge the region to participate in a Regional Peace and Development Programme, which includes an agreement by all the countries in the region 'to resolve their differences peacefully', in accordance with a Code of Agreement, using mediation and conciliation organizations in the UN, or elsewhere, and (if necessary) asking UN peacekeeping troops to help the process. Assurances safeguarding human rights, backed by regional courts and monitored by the Regional Secretariat could also encourage a stable and peaceful region.

The problem facing Vietnam in Kampuchea is well described by David Bull in an Oxfam booklet, *The Poverty of Diplomacy, Kampuchea and the Outside World*, in which he asserts:

> Peace and stability for the Khmer people means primarily an end to the threat from the Khmers and to the border conflict. This is a strangely illogical war in which even the Western nations that back the Coalition at the UN say they don't want them ever to win. The Coalition, they say, is supported in order to persuade the Vietnamese to leave Kampuchea, yet their support seems to have exactly the opposite effect. As long as the Khmer Rouge cast their shadow over the country, the Vietnamese are likely to remain and the Kampuchean people will be glad of their protection.....The present ban on development aid does nothing to bring about a political settlement and condemns the Khmer people to a long-term insufficiency and even continued malnutrition and ill-health predicted by the UN's own surveys.

Considering that the Kampuchean people are victims of a war over which they have no control it may be thought our compassion for their sufferings would at least have encouraged us to give emergency aid, but even this help is being denied because of American and Chinese pressure, while military assistance through Thailand continues. What a different situation there could have been if the promise (soon to be forgotten, alas) of massive economic aid to Vietnam made by the USA towards the end of the Vietnam war had been fulfilled.

This region could be a promising area in which to promote USA/USSR/Chinese co-operation. If these nations agreed to support a Regional Peace and Development Programme it could become operational immediately and go a long way towards promoting trust and confidence between them, possibly with far reaching results in other parts of the world.

Another alternative source of funds could be found in countries bordering S.E.Asia, i.e. Japan, Australia, New Zealand, and the Asian countries. Between them they could provide adequate funds and in doing so resolve a dangerous situation which threatens to poison the region for a long time to come. Japan in particular has a responsibility because (like Europe) it received economic aid from the USA after the war and today has a massive balance of payments surplus which threatens the economic stability of the whole world. A generous gesture to S.E.Asia could do much to restore the region to social, economic and political stability and provide Japan with the opportunity to become a world leader towards the ideal of a world at peace. With her past experience of nuclear war and her embarrassingly large international credits, she could be the ideal nation to take the lead by encouraging Regional Peace and Development in the region which is in her own 'backyard'.

It is also ironic that we in the Western world are prepared to spend many millions of pounds helping the Vietnamese Boat People resettle in the West, yet are not prepared to spend a similar amount to help them rehabilitate in their own country. It would be interesting to know what the total financial cost of resettling the thousands of Boat People has been, because, if everything were taken into consideration, including education, housing, social security payments, transport, etc., etc. in the USA, Britain, and many other parts of the world, the total cost of helping them must run into several hundred millions of pounds. In addition there is the burden of the refugee camps in Thailand and Hong Kong which again must run into several millions of pounds a year and promises to continue into the distant future creating resentment and injustice in the process. How much more cost-effective and more satisfactory in every way it would have been to have used this money instead to promote a regional development programme; the problem would then have been resolved permanently at its source.

THE HORN OF AFRICA

Thanks to Bob Geldof the tragedy of Ethiopia is well known to all of us. What is not so well known is that the tragedy is largely man-made and largely the result of war. First conquered by Italy in 1936, then liberated by the British in 1940; then, following the end of the Second World War, continual war against Eritrea, supported in turn by the USSR and the USA each using Ethiopia as a pawn in their search for a power base. Even now (1988) the war continues with no end in sight, depleting the country of essentials of every kind and causing relief supplies to be burned on the lorries taking relief food.

The cost to Ethiopia in human suffering is immense, but so too must be the cost in financial terms to the rich nations of the world. The armaments poured into Ethiopia, by the USA and the USSR, without any real hope of payment, must be enormous while the cost of helping with emergency aid must also be considerable, all of which is not dealing with the cause of the problem which is the war itself.

61

Short-term emergency aid must be given to the millions dying of starvation, but to continue to do so without seeking to end the war will only relieve the immediate suffering but do little to remove the cause. Development therefore should be offered on a regional basis, including South Sudan which is accommodating so many refugees. A regional Peace and Development Programme should be made available for Eritrea, Somalia, Ethiopia and South Sudan in accordance with the Code of Agreement detailed elsewhere in this Proposal.

The Horn of Africa would be an ideal region for USA/USSR co-operation. Both these countries have by now surely begun to realize the futility of trying to compete with each other for a sphere of influence in Ethiopia and should recognise the gains that could be made from co-operation. For a fraction of the money spent supporting war in the region, peace and stability could be found.

Failing funds being found from the Great Powers, there are other sources available such as Europe, Scandinavia, Japan, and the oil-rich countries. Provided there was the political will these countries could find sufficient funds for the Horn of Africa. The amount of money needed, in Ethiopian terms, to restore the region to one of peace and prosperity will be considerable, but negligible in world terms.

Aid should be given on a regional basis on the understanding that prior agreement is reached on social, economic and political issues, particularly that the region makes every endeavour to achieve a peaceful resolution of its conflicts by every means possible and initiates a Regional Convention of Human Rights and a Regional Court of Human Rights.

SOUTHERN AFRICA

The Southern African Development Conference countries (embracing Angola, Zambia, Botswana, Zimbabwe, Mozambique, Lesotho, Malawi, Swaziland, and Tanzania), is already a recognised region and is attempting to attract $2 billion over ten years for regional development to gain economic liberation from South Africa. This has driven them to direct their whole effort to the struggle for political and economic independence from South Africa with the result that they take one step forward but two back in their struggle for economic recovery. Probably only economic support from the outside world encouraging economic, social and political co-operation to the whole of the region, including

South Africa, by the offer of a Regional Peace and Development Programme, can break this deadlock and bring peaceful conditions to the region as a whole.

Alternatively, a smaller region consisting of South Africa with only its immediate neighbours may be easier and less costly to initiate. These countries could be: Angola, Namibia, Botswana, Zambia, Mozambique and the two countries within South Africa, Lesotho and Swaziland.

At first sight it may appear that these regions have too many problems to be suitable for a Regional Peace and Development Programme, but it is precisely because of the crisis in the area which makes it suitable, for the following reasons:

1. If present trends continue the white population in South Africa will stand to lose everything in a civil war: so too will the rich countries with investments there. Thus there is a strong incentive for them to support a Regional Peace and Development Programme, even if the concessions on human rights, demanded in a Code of Agreement, prove difficult for the South African government to accept.
2. The Code of Agreement, in addition to safeguarding the social, economic and political human rights of the Blacks, would also safeguard these same human rights for the Whites, and thus remove one of their main fears of Black rule. As a further incentive for acceptance by the Whites in South Africa the Regional Peace and Development Programme could be phased over a 5 – 10 year period alongside a clearly defined agreement for a step by step process towards democracy and a firm commitment to safeguard human rights, monitored by the Regional Secretariat.[5]
3. The injection of adequate money from an international fund to ensure good development for the poorest populations in the region would also indirectly increase the prosperity of the Whites and thus be an added incentive for them to accept the Code of Agreement.
4. Peaceful conditions in the region would release vast sums of money, currently being used for war purposes by both Blacks and Whites.
5. The African National Congress has already committed itself to promoting social, economic and political human rights and has assured

---

5. See chapter dealing with the 'Code of Agreement', page 21

the Whites of equal rights under the law. There should therefore be no difficulty in encouraging co-operation between Whites and Blacks in a Regional Peace and Development Programme, especially if economic aid is directed specifically at helping the rural economies of the poor countries, and human rights are included as an essential part of the Code of Agreement.[6]

6. Sanctions are often thought to be the only way to make the South African government abolish apartheid, but they can be counter-productive. Not only may sanctions entrench White opinion, making them fearful about 'giving in' after many years of hard work, but the government is forced to encourage a siege economy to make the country more self-sufficient and less vulnerable to sanctions. If sanctions therefore only have a limited value, and the prospect of civil war is unacceptable, dire necessity should demand that attempts to obtain agreement between the ANC and the South African government for a Regional Peace and Development Programme should be made. Sooner or later an agreement will have to be made with South Africa; it would be much better to seek one now before conditions deteriorate even further. The initiative must lie with the rich nations who have the necessary resources.

7. Many Whites are acutely aware of the dangers facing their country but are unable to make their voices clearly heard because they do not have the economic power to offer a convincing policy to counter the fears of the majority; it is therefore difficult for them to influence and possibly change their government. A constructive Regional Peace and Development Programme could provide this alternative and thus help and encourage minority progressive forces to become the majority. There is no guarantee they will succeed but unless they are given support they are probably fighting a losing battle. The belief that the White population would accept a Regional Peace and Development Programme is supported by a White correspondent who has lived and worked in Southern Africa for 13 years; he writes: 'I consider your proposals by far

---

6. See page 116 for details of a proposal made by a Southern African inter-racial group called Groundswell. This group has just published a book making suggestions similar to the Regional Peace and Development Programme

the most sensible and constructive in the frightful and worsening situation'.

8. It may be argued that there can be no guarantee that a Regional Peace and Development Programme will succeed. This criticism would perhaps be valid if aid was given to individual nations or without any prior agreement about how it was to be administered or used. This objection could be overcome by insisting on a *regional* concept within an agreed Code of Agreement, implemented over a five to ten year period during which time it would be monitored by a Regional Secretariat who could stop all aid if the spirit of the Code was not observed. This means that acceptance of the Code would provide some assurance of success to the rich countries who are providing the funds, and assurance to the recipients in the region that their ideals can be attained. If, however, the region as a whole cannot agree to the terms of the Code then no funds would be involved. Thus there is every reason for offering a Regional Peace and Development Programme.

SOUTHERN AMERICA

The war in the Falklands has brought into focus the need for a Regional Peace and Development Programme to include Argentina and Chile. This region has been notoriously unstable with poverty and dictatorships ruling for many years. Human rights have been ignored with tyranny and torture commonplace. Fortunately, in recent years a new democratic government has emerged in Argentina but it is carrying an immense burden of debt incurred by the previous government. There can therefore be no assurance that the government will survive for long unless help is given.

The future of the Falklanders is also in doubt because it is difficult to believe that the present situation can rely for ever on the British army, navy and air force to protect it. The cost to Britain of an indefinite stay will be too great to bear and therefore some other permanent solution must be found. The solution could be the offer of a Regional Peace and Development Programme for Chile, Argentina and the Falklands.

A Regional Peace and Development Programme would be attractive to all concerned; to Argentina and Chile by encouraging their sluggish economies to revive, and to the Falklands by offering them a secure economic future within a community which respects human rights. The future economy of the Falklands must also rest with Argentina and Chile because these nations are her nearest neighbours and other nations, especially Britain, are too far away. A regional agreement with these countries therefore makes good economic sense.

The future of the Falklanders could be further safeguarded by a step by step approach towards independence under UN auspices. By including the Falklands within a Southern American Community it should be possible for honour to be satisfied on all sides and goodwill established within a regional economic, social and political framework. This is the essential criterion upon which the future of the Falklanders must rest; their future cannot be assured by a defence concept which implicitly denies co-operation while incurring vast expenditure over an indefinite period. If the development programme were spread over a five to ten year period, while monitored by a Regional Secretariat, with social, economic and political human rights assured, it is reasonable to believe that the changed social environment would gradually lead to agreement about the future of the Falklands. Until then the island could remain a UN Trustee with its freedoms assured by reason of the fact that if Argentina threatened invasion all regional development aid would cease.

The cost, if Britain alone attempted to offer the development programme, would be high, but probably less than the estimated three or four billion pounds already spent defending the Falklands. The cost would be tempered by the knowledge that a Regional Peace and Development Programme would relieve the banking world of the fear that Argentina and Chile would default on their debts; the banking world would also gain from increased trade and banking services. A regional programme would therefore offer a permanent solution to the debt problem in Southern America.

A Regional Peace and Development Programme should be initiated in Southern America on humanitarian grounds alone in view of the ill-treatment being shown to the people of Chile and the fear that Argentina may yet lapse into the same situation. The main attraction to Britain of a regional solution however would be that it would provide a long-term solution to the Falklands problem possibly at less cost than the present Fortress Falklands policy. An initiative by Britain could encourage other countries to participate.

CENTRAL AMERICA

Nine countries in Central America have for several years been striving to promote a regional agreement to resolve the conflicts in this part of the world. Unfortunately, instead of helping these countries to co-operate and become a Central American Community, the US Government seems intent on preventing it happening by encouraging right-wing elements in El Salvador and Nicaragua with military equipment and other support. The result is that the region is becoming more and more destabilised with anti-American feelings increasing not only in Central America, but around the world.

Resolving the problems of Central America must depend primarily on the USA because of its proximity and close involvement with the region. However, it is surely right for us to ask the USA to use the golden opportunity provided by the voluntary coming together of Mexico, Columbia, Venezuela, Panama, Honduras, Costa Rica, Guatemala, El Salvador and Nicaragua to initiate a Marshall Plan for the region. The basic problems which prompted the USA to help Europe in 1946 are being reproduced in Central America and they should be resolved in a similar manner.

Alas, the USA has a blind spot here and is obsessed with defeating communism by every means and in doing so is encouraging the very problem it is seeking to overcome. If the same effort now being devoted to 'destroying communism' were to be employed in promoting a Regional Peace and Development Programme, the security of the region, and of the USA, could be assured.

Ideally, a Central American Regional Peace and Development Programme should be financed by the UN through a new UN Peace and Development Fund. The European Community has already expressed its support for the Contadora Group and may be willing to support it financially, especially if the USA took the lead by first making a contribution.

A regional initiative should also be welcomed by the US Government because it would ensure basic human rights to all, with freedom under the law, ideals which it claims to be supporting around the world. It should also be welcomed because it is essential for the USA to have a stable and prosperous region on its doorstep. But no attempt should be made to change the nature of any government, because that is each country's own internal affair, but the region as a whole would be encouraged to promote respect for social, economic and political justice based on the UN Universal Declaration of Human Rights. If such an initiative were made, instead of the region being seen as a threat to the USA, it could become a stable and prosperous friend.

All the indications currently are that the region would welcome a Regional Peace and Development Programme along the lines proposed in the Code of Agreement. Writing about the Central American Peace Plan Maurice Walsh in *The Guardian* of August 10th 1987 emphasizes the need when he says:

> Even if a ceasefire is successfully negotiated and the warring parties begin to develop the changes outlined in the agreement (in the Central American Peace Plan), *the region's economic problems will remain chronic and impervious to a healthy recovery without outside assistance*.

THE SOUTH PACIFIC ISLAND STATES

Initiating a Regional Peace and Development Programme for this region should present little difficulty in financial terms because the total number of people involved is small, numbering only about two million. A Regional Community is needed because each island is so small it needs the support of the others, especially now that they are gaining independence from colonial governments. The financial cost of promoting a South Pacific Regional Peace and Development Programme therefore should present little difficulty.

The major question, however, is how to stop the so-called 'Great Powers' from using the region as a testing ground for nuclear weapons. The region itself desperately wants to become a nuclear-free zone, as the South Pacific Nuclear Free Zone Treaty indicates. This Treaty was signed by eight members in 1985 but now (1987) has been increased to 13 members, including Australia and New Zealand, but not by Britain, France, the USA and Japan who all want to retain the right to use the region as a dumping ground for nuclear waste, or for testing their nuclear bombs, or for retaining strategic naval bases.

Recently, further attempts (in the Treaty of Rarotonga) have been made to strengthen and enlarge the concept of a nuclear-free zone and although Britain, France and the USA have failed to sign the Treaty, the USSR has signed thus providing the USSR with an easy political gain. If the West ignores the legitimate demands of the Pacific Islanders by continuing to test nuclear bombs, demanding naval bases and dumping their nuclear wastes, the time will come when the USSR gains all the Islanders' support at the expense of the West. Once again short-term gain may lead to a long-term loss.

The refusal by the West to support a nuclear-free zone, however, need not prevent a Regional Peace and Development Programme being initiated immediately. The region has already demonstrated amply its desire to rid itself of nuclear involvement.

The reason the South Pacific is included in this suggested list of suitable regions is because the cost to the world community would be negligible, and because the trend towards co-operation is strong and needs our support. Also many of the islands are poor and need our help. Above all it would enable the first step towards world peace to be taken soon and provide an example to the world.

SRI LANKA

Although Sri Lanka is an island and not a region, it is nevertheless a country eminently suited to a Regional Peace and Development Programme. This is because its small size would enable the programme to be initiated quickly, and also because the nation has a poor population with divided loyalties. The cost of a development programme would be comparatively small for the rich nations to bear and should not present insuperable financial difficulties.

It is not for 'outsiders' to seek to impose a solution to the conflict on the island because the answer must be found by the people, helped, however, by the incentive of a Regional Peace and Development Programme which would provide the means by which the Tamils and Sinhalese, for their mutual benefit, could agree a Code of Agreement supporting social, economic and political human rights.

These are objectives to which everyone on the island can agree. They should also be able to agree to use the good offices of the UN mediators, or other Non-Government Organization mediators to reach an agreement, or, if necessary request the presence of

69

UN Peace-keeping Forces to calm the situation during the early stages.

It is not suggested that a development programme should be 'open-ended' but that it should be conditional on the different ethnic groups 'making every effort to reach agreement'. If it became evident that the two opposing sides in the present dispute were failing to 'make every effort' then the help should be withdrawn.

REPUBLIC OF IRELAND AND NORTHERN IRELAND

As with Sri Lanka, this is an island with divided loyalties which can perhaps only be resolved if there is a willingness between the conflicting parties to seek agreement. A Regional Peace and Development Programme could provide the required incentive for Northern Ireland and the Republic of Ireland to co-operate for their mutual benefit by helping them to promote a healthy social and economic environment in which mutual trust and confidence may be nurtured.

The conflict in Northern Ireland is costing Britain dear in financial and social terms. The cost of maintaining an armed presence there and subsidizing the economic base of the country (with unemployment the highest in the British Isles), plus the cost of disruption to the economy by continual conflict must be enormous. There is also intangible cost resulting from the loss of moral leadership to the detriment of Britain's good name around the world. Some of this expenditure should immediately be used to deal with the root causes of the problem by initiating a UN Peace and Development Fund. Such a Fund could attract some of the hundred million dollars reported to have been given by the USA to help reconcile Northern Ireland with the Republic of Ireland. This gift, though well meant, was given without being integrated within a well-structured organization and will probably fail in its objective.

As both the Republic and Northern Ireland are members of the EEC and the Commonwealth, it seems reasonable to hope that if a Regional Peace and Development Programme for all Ireland programme were initiated it would attract financial help from both these organizations.

It would be important for a Peace and Development Fund to be under the auspices of the UN as an independent body. The

Commonwealth or the EEC could administer and monitor the programme successfully.

THE MIDDLE EAST

The Middle East is perhaps potentially the most explosive region in the world, yet if a Regional Peace and Development Programme could be made available, which ensured social, economic and political human rights, the Arabs and Israelis may learn the arts of reconciliation in the same way that the war-time Allies have learnt to live in peace with the Germans, encouraged by the Marshall Plan, after the last war.

This idea is not as far-fetched as it may, at first, appear because the Israeli Prime Minister (according to a report in *Forum*, the Council of Europe's official journal), in a speech to the European Parliament in February 1986, suggested the idea of a 'Marshall Plan' for the Middle East.

The attraction of a Regional Peace and Development Programme for Lebanon, Syria, and Jordan must be considerable in view of the devastation of this area in recent years. Israel too must long for the day when she can live at peace with her neighbours and would probably be prepared to make some sacrifices to make this hope a reality.

This process towards reconciliation could be further encouraged if some of the money at present given to Israel and the Arabs to support their wars was redirected into a UN Peace and Development Fund, earmarked for a Middle East Regional Peace and Development Programme. This would give the incentive for all parties to reach a common understanding, based on supporting social, economic and political human rights for both the Israelis and Arabs. Financial support for such a programme could also be sought from the oil-rich nations, support which is at present being given to help the Arabs in their fight against Israel.

Both the Arabs and the Israelis need the intervention of a neutral body such as the UN, with adequate resources at its disposal, to restore the economy and social framework of the region. It is probably impossible to find a solution to the present dispute while the social and economic conditions are so chaotic and passions run so high. Therefore a period of time is needed to allow feelings to calm down and to allow reconstruction to take place within an agreed Code of Agreement.

71

While it is unlikely a solution can be found until passions are reduced, it should be possible to insist on a Code of Agreement requiring all parties to show a 'determination to seek peaceful relationships' and to 'respect human rights'. Evidence of this determination would be needed by a Regional Secretariat who could encourage the use of a UN Conciliation or NGO body, and the UN Peacekeeping Force to find a regional solution, a solution which cannot be imposed but must come from within the region itself.

This process towards reconciliation could be further encouraged if the Israelis and Arabs knew that in future the USA and the oil states were to redirect a proportion of the present help they give to finance their wars to support a Regional Peace and Development Programme.

A UN solution along the above lines also could invite support from the rest of the world, including the Communist bloc. A peaceful resolution of the Middle East problem must appeal to the Russians because it cannot be in her interests to have continual conflict so near her borders. A financial contribution from Russia would also help towards USSR/USA *rapprochement* and could lead them to further co-operation in other regions of the world. Acts of co-operation of this kind would be far more cost effective in preserving their security, freedoms and human rights than all the threatening postures now employed involving a huge defence expenditure.

The USA/USSR Summit meeting in Washington, at which they signed their historic Intermediate Nuclear Forces treaty (INF) on November 8th 1987, has led to further co-operation in Moscow when President Regan and Mr Gorbachev met in 1988. Already they are agreed that human rights and the problems in the regions will be high on their agenda. Instead of seeking to score points off each other in Afghanistan and Central America they must be encouraged to seek a comprehensive long-term agreement through the UN by initiating a UN Peace and Development Fund to promote Regional Peace and Development Programmes as outlined in this book, for these and other regions.

World Security

International Law—Its basis and its future

It is probably true to say that everyone wants peace, especially in this nuclear age, but we differ radically about how it may be achieved. On the one side are those who believe in armed resistance, or the concept of deterrence; on the other, are the unilateralists who reject the idea of nuclear war. These two differing views divide us when it is not necessary; instead we could find unity in a positive creative approach about which we can all agree.

This chapter therefore seeks to understand a third alternative based on understanding the relationship between development, international law, and security. If this purpose could be perceived and understood then development programmes could be specifically conceived to achieve this objective within the United Nations.

Another reason for this chapter is because once the relationship between development, law, and peace is understood, the political will to implement programmes will follow. This chapter therefore seeks to understand the nature of law based on forces other than violence and finds the answer rests on the concept of justice and a sense of fairness arising from our total environment. Our task therefore is to promote social, economic and political justice because only when these are seen and felt to be in accordance with our sense of fairness will support for law be given. We should seek a world society by methods which not only remove the causes of war but also, by the same means, promotes the basis of good law, law which is effective because it is respected. It is not a quick, easy answer but once it is seen to be the objective, makes it possible for us to understand why a vast range of positive creative steps can promote justice and lead to world security and world peace.

Consequently, my proposition is that a regional approach to the problem is the best way of dealing with the problem in today's situation.

The Environment and Law

The belief in a favourable environment was well expressed in Sir Herbert Read's chapter The Arts and Peace (in *Alternatives to War and Violence* p 161) in which he says:

> Plato 'always insisted on the profound effects of environment....that ideas do not change men; they are changed by physical forces only....the mind...should be overwhelmed with harmonic sights and sounds...for this reason ..education must always be total'.

This quotation is given because it is not always appreciated that our behaviour is dictated more by our feelings, which arise from the nature of our environment, than by learned argument. Our search for peace and security therefore demands that we understand the nature of our environment within a total ecological approach to the problem.

This theme about the nature of our environment is supported by Aristotle (as reported in Dr. Cowen's book *The Foundations of Freedom* (Oxford University Press 1961) as saying the law must be 'in accordance with nature'; and Cicero when he says, 'true law is right reason in agreement with nature'.

The search for the basis of law continued over the following centuries with St. Augustine in the 5th century and St. Thomas Aquinas in the 13th century being important influences. Their thinking may be summed up by quotation from Henry Bracton in the Introduction to Dr. Cowen's book:

> The king ought not to be under any man, but ought to be under God and the law, since the law makes the king. Therefore let the king render unto the law what the law has rendered unto the king, namely dominion and power; for there is no king where will prevails but not the law.

This fundamental idea, that governments must be under God and the moral law, or the law itself soon degenerates into unfettered power is equally applicable today because unfettered power without consent and justice soon degenerates into tyranny. In other words, to refer back to the legal maxim asserted by the stoic philosphers, 'An unjust law is not law' (p. 22 of *The Lawful Rights of Mankind* by Paul Sieghart, Oxford University Press 1986).

Later still, in the 17th century, Grotius founded what is now regarded as the modern science of international law. (Professor Norman Bentwich summarizes Grotius's views in his chapter The Basis of International Law in World Affairs in *Alternatives to War and Violence* p. 74[1] as:

> Grotius believed in a Law of Nature which supplements, and sometimes over-rides the customary law of nations. 'It was composed of the dictates of right reason, which pointed out the act according as it is, or is not, in conformity with nature, and has a quality of moral baseness or moral necessity, and therefore is either forbidden, or enjoyed by God, the author of nature.'

This idea that positive law has a relationship with the moral law, based on a belief in God, Nature or Reason, has been supported by many philosophers and writers who believed in the idea of law from the time of Plato to the present day.

Reason and Law

Many outstanding contributions were made in the following years by writers such as Bentham, Locke and Rousseau, with their emphasis placed on reason, justice and human rights and the inspiring idea of a social contract. All these concepts, while in accordance with the idea of Natural Law, inadequately take into account the importance of our environment and our spiritual well-being in making decisions. Reason and justice are intellectual concepts which cannot convince those whose passions and feelings have been aroused by social or economic abuses. Our task therefore is to address ourselves to changing the nature of society so that our feelings are in harmony with our environment. This is the task of reason and why the idea of justice is so vitally important. It is also the basic philosophy of Natural Law.

During the 18th century the concept of Natural Law fell into disrepute and only in recent years has the concept again begun to be taken seriously. This change may have profound repercussions on our whole approach to international relationships; without a clear

---

1. See Bibliography

sense of direction, our politicians, who make the law, have allowed science to dictate our future, not by deliberate intent, but because the philosophy guiding the country has been shaped by materialistic and militaristic ends. Consequently, instead of science being our slave, it threatens to become our master. The concept of Natural Law is also seriously neglected by the peace movement when it could be providing the movement's philosophical basis and consequent motive power for all activities.

The Church and the Law

This decline in belief in Natural Law was accelerated because the Catholic Church in the fifteenth and sixteenth centuries so abused its power that it obscured the essential nature of belief, including the sense of wonder in the miracle of life and belief in something beyond our understanding but which many of us call God and others the Inner Light, Great Spirit or the Ultimate. It was also a period of time which coincided with the availability of the printed word which allowed people, for the first time, the opportunity to read and discover for themselves the falsities and hypocrisy of much of the Church's teachings. In this way the baby of belief was thrown out with the dirty water of the institutionalized Roman Church instead of obeying the spirit and teaching of Jesus. This revolt against the authority of the Church subsequently became known as the Reformation and gave birth to Non-conformity.

If only the Church had taken more notice of its great thinkers over the centuries, men such as St. Augustine, St. Thomas Aquinas, Thomas à Kempis and Rousseau instead of taking the path of power and wealth. Fortunately the Catholic Church in recent years has shown itself more in tune with the concept of Natural Law through writers such as Pierre Teilhard de Chardin and Thomas Merton and especially Pope John's great encyclical *Pacem in Terris* in 1963.

Disillusionment with the Church and the availability of the printed word also encouraged many to believe that science, reason, and logic alone could conquer nature and lead us to Utopia. It appeared that speculation about the nature of God was almost an impediment to any search for peace and well-being. The consequence of this divorce between man and Nature is that we have since been engaged in a battle against Nature, instead of a partnership with Her. This attitude of killing anything which threatens human well-being has influenced almost every aspect of life where disease is concerned and far too little attention is given to removing the causes of ill health by promoting positive health.

We have arrogantly neglected the first principle of life, that unless we live in harmony with our environment Nature will destroy us, even though we may sometimes achieve startling successes in the short term. War should be regarded as a disease and peace a natural outcome of a healthy world order. We may learn to fly, for instance, but we can only defy gravity for a short period on the principle that what goes up must come down. In so many ways we are defying the natural order and unless we learn to manage the world more successfully than at present a crash is inevitable. It is a race against time to learn humility, to listen to the promptings of conscience, and to live by wisdom and an understanding of the natural world. Science and knowledge must be harnessed to this central understanding and not left to take us to the abyss of total annihilation. If, on the other hand, science and education teach us to live in harmony with our environment we have it well within our power to avoid this catastrophe. We may not be able to abolish conflict situations, but at least we can learn to ritualize them without killing each other.

Many of our problems arise because of our difficulties with language meaning different beliefs to each of us. This applies particularly to words such as, 'God' and 'Natural Law'. Different interpretations or assumptions of these words have provoked misunderstandings and even wars. The very mention of the words God, or Love for instance, instantly turn many people's minds away from the subject which is being discussed. This has led to the idea of God being officially outlawed, as in Communist countries, and being almost ignored in the democracies. This state of affairs has suited some governments because a passive Church without a strong social and political conscience has been welcomed. Jesus's two essential commandments; first to love God (especially obedience to the Natural Order as perceived in Nature) and secondly to love our neighbour, could provide the means of unifying peoples of all nations and all religions while still leaving each nation and each religion free to worship in its own way. Unfortunately dogma all too often obscures the way to a world of unity with diversity. Surely we can all agree on first principles while allowing each of us to worship in his or her own way?

Darwin, Science and the Law

The tendency to look to science for guidance was encouraged by Darwin's famous book, *The Origin of Species*. The ideas in this work coincided with the prevailing competitive and materialistic mood of the time, and because Darwin's work was portrayed, probably falsely, as a denial of the concept of God, the popular belief was encouraged that science could solve all our problems. Unfortunately this popular move away from belief in a power beyond ourselves left science without any guiding principles to ensure that it is directed towards the good of mankind, the result being that we now find ourselves dominated by forces beyond our control. It has also meant that the opportunity to harness the spiritual forces of mankind, which could transform the world, has been lost. Science is neutral but can be a blessing or curse depending on how it is directed and used.

Darwin's theory, that survival depends on being, or becoming, the fittest, was exploited by the rich and militaristic world to support their belief in the competitive society, despite protestations from Darwin's friend, Alfred Russel Wallace (who some claim was co-author of the theory of Natural Selection) that this interpretation was, if not false, a gross over-simplification. Darwin did not join in the controversy but Wallace, who was a noted naturalist, biologist and social reformer, believed that co-operation was the key to our survival. His detailed researches, with supporting evidence about the natural world, were brushed aside as of little importance by a public that did not want to know. Wallace was a man before his time, being a passionate advocate of views radically different from Victorian materialism, but which are, belatedly, being recognised today as important truths. Wallace argued (according to his biographer Harry Clements, in *Alfred Russel Wallace*, Hutchinson, 1983) that 'Mind and Spirit uniquely enabled man to modify the effects of natural selection.' He then quotes Wallace as saying:

> ...from the moment the first skin was used as a covering, when the first rude spear was formed to assist him in the chase, when fire was first used to cook his food, the first seed or shoot planted, a grand revolution was effected in Nature—a revolution which in all previous ages of the earth's history has no parallel. A being had arisen who was no longer subject to bodily change with changes in the physical universe—a being who was in some degree superior to Nature, inasmuch as he knew how to control her action and could keep

himself in harmony with her, not through any change in his body, but by
means of a vast superiority of mind.

Despite the many threats to life on earth which science has brought
it has also given us immense power and knowledge so that we now
enjoy a standard of living beyond the dreams of previous generations.
But although science is of enormous importance, unless it is guided by
wisdom, patience, understanding and intellectual honesty in accordance
with the concept of Natural Law and natural laws, it will lead us to our
destruction.

An analogy with the Highway Code may be applicable. We all
usually wish to travel from A to B as quickly as possible but recognise
that to do so we must obey certain rules, such as keeping to one or
other side of the road, stopping at traffic lights, etc. etc. These rules
are a limitation on our personal liberties but we accept them because
they are recognised to be in accordance with our sense of fairness,
natural justice or Natural Law. A badly designed road or crossing, or
an inadequate road for the traffic, will lead to frustration, chaos, bad
temper and conflict, with the probability that the law will be infringed.
Similar rules apply to international relationships; if we wish to reach
the ideal of peace we must first map out the direction we want to go
and then be willing to sacrifice a small degree of personal freedom in
order to reach our destination.

Fortunately in recent years, especially in the USA and Scandinavia,
the concept of Natural Law is once again being seriously considered by
international lawyers to be of fundamental importance to international
law. Lord Lloyd of Hampstead, Q.C. in his recently revised standard
textbook *Introduction to Jurisprudence*, (Stevens, 1985) emphasises
this point in his preface when he says,

> We have in this edition given much greater attention to both the history
> and philosophy of natural law thinking. This chapter is nearly three times
> the length as in the previous edition.

Perhaps the day is dawning when our search for truth will reveal
the nature of God through the sciences, especially the sciences
dealing with the nature of our environment in relationship to human
behaviour. The teachings of the priest-scientist Teilhard de Chardin,
the psychologist Jung, the contemporary scientist Fritjof Capra, and
famous international lawyers such as Finnis and Rawls, for example,

are beginning to have real influence. So much so that it may only be a matter of time before another revolution in mankind's thinking will take place. But time is not on our side; in the meanwhile it is imperative for us to take the first step towards sanity in one of the regions of the world in accordance with our present understanding of relationships between ourselves and our environment.

Despite the obvious perils the world now faces, caused by science travelling too fast along a road without any clear sense of moral direction, tremendous advances have been made as a result of mankind's search for truth, in both the political and the scientific world, which, if only we gave them a sense of moral direction, could rescue us from most of our troubles, especially hunger and poverty and the fear of war. Unfortunately governments do not possess the political will, vision and wisdom to act in accordance with moral values and have embraced a philosophy based on suppressive acts which, at best, can only be palliative; on the other hand, support for concepts based on promoting a healthy society, and a healthy world order is given grudgingly and receives scant resources.

Defence can command almost unlimited resources but peacemaking and the prevention of war by other means almost nothing; even the Department of Development in East Anglia's University (probably Britain's most important research department for development studies) is threatened with closure, while Peace Studies are viewed with open hostility. The philosophy of war preparation and that of war prevention, reconciliation and conciliation, including the idea of security under the rule of law, are poles apart. Unfortunately both compete for the same financial resources and therefore a choice has to be made as to which path we want to take; to prepare for war, or to prepare for peace. Fortunately the choice can be implemented step by step by promoting economic, social and political justice in the regions of the world whenever possible, but a conscious choice has to be made about the long-term aim.

Regional Organizations and the Law

Giant strides have been made however, in many directions which, if understood, and integrated within regional structures globally could resolve many of our problems. For instance, issues calling for action with regard to regional co-operation brought to the attention of the UN

Economic and Social Council (in a Report of the Secretary-General in June 1986) included the need for Regional Social and Economic Commissions for Asia and the Pacific, for Latin America and the Caribbean, and for Africa and Western Asia.

Attempts to implement human rights in the American and African continents have also found expression in the American Declaration of Rights and Duties of Man, the Inter-American Convention of Human Rights and the African Charter on Human and People's Rights. These splendid documents, especially the Inter-American Convention of Human Rights in which 12 states have agreed to be legally bound all indicate the wish to make human rights enforceable. Regrettably these states have not yet found it possible to achieve the necessary degree of trust and confidence between themselves to enable them to establish effective regional courts of human rights with the express power to deliver binding judgements against individual states. What is still lacking in all regions, other than the European, is the social, economic and political structure for regional co-operation, such as Regional Peace and Development could provide.

The most important advance in regional co-operation and the rule of law however is to be found in the European Convention on Human Rights. It is perhaps pertinent to observe that although the European countries have a long history of hostility and war, the experience of co-operating within the Marshall Plan encouraged Europeans to initiate the Council of Europe and soon afterwards to formulate the European Convention on Human Rights. The European Convention was followed by a Protocol and Charter covering civil and political rights and a wide range of economic, social and cultural rights. These were adopted in 1961 and entered into force in 1965. Paul Sieghart, writing in his book *The Lawful Rights of Mankind* (Oxford University Press 1965 p. 67) about the European Convention says:

> ..it seems nothing short of miraculous that the sovereign member states of the Council of Europe were willing in such a short time, to set up wholly independent institutions—a European Commission of Human Rights, and a European Court of Human Rights, both sitting in Strasbourg—outside the political or administrative control of any of them, which would have the competence and the power to sit in judgement on them over precisely these issues. More remarkable still, proceedings before these institutions can be begun not only by other states, but by *individuals* against any state that has made an appropriate declaration recognizing the competence of the Commission to entertain

such proceedings. And the European Court of Human Rights, to which cases may be referred after the Commission has investigated them, has express power to deliver *binding* judgements against the states concerned in the proceedings. All this amounts to a substantial retreat from the previously sacred principle of national sovereignty, as a necessary price for at long last including human rights in the area of *legitimate* international concern.

This remarkable progress gives us encouragement to believe that effective international law is not an impossible dream but something which is within our grasp if only the necessary steps are taken to ensure social and economic well-being such as are proposed in the idea of Regional Peace and Development Programmes.

Thanks to the Council of Europe, the nations of Western Europe have learnt to co-operate and accept the disciplines which co-operation brings to attain the goals of freedom under the law, and are now willing to accept the jurisdiction of a European Court of Human Rights with power to enforce its decisions over any of its member states. Up to 1983 some 60 cases had been brought before the Court including issues such as the use of corporal punishment; trade union freedoms to bargain collectively; controls of telephone tapping; the principle of presumption of innocence in criminal proceedings. This willingness to sacrifice a small degree of national sovereignty for the good of all has grown organically, almost absent-mindedly, as a natural outcome of co-operation and confirms the ideas of Plato, quoted earlier, about the 'profound effects of the environment...being overwhelmed with harmonic sights and sounds...education must be total'.

The speech by George C. Marshall, the Secretary of State to the USA, which inaugurated the Marshall Plan, forecast one of the most imaginative and far-seeing political acts in modern history and set in motion the idea for European unity. It is, however, an idea still in its infancy, evolving and uncertain whether to take the path of violence, or the path of life; whether to seek to become a world power with all its militaristic implications, or a world power by reason of its authority based on economic and social justice, respect for human rights, and the moral leadership it could give to the rest of the world in support of the rule of law between nations. It is to be hoped the progress being made in the Council of Europe's institutions will prevail over the idea of a militaristic Western Union, as is sometimes urged. The question as to where Europe is going is still not resolved. For many it is the means to

obtain power so as to emulate the other two Great Powers in the belief
that it will lead to a Europe with more effective muscle in the political
world. The alternative is a Europe providing an example of social and
economic justice under the rule of law, but of law founded on very
different foundations from that of violence. The role of the European
Economic Community should therefore be subordinated to that of the
Council of Europe. There is no doubt that economic co-operation
demands adequate machinery to enable it to function efficiently
with adequate funds at its disposal to promote positive regional
development, but the danger is that once economic and political power
is concentrated, it can so easily be misused to the detriment of others.
Many politicians in Britain for instance have expressly supported entry
into Europe primarily to enable Britain to become another Great Power,
including being a military power so that our influence may be more
effective. Such an outcome could only result in an even more unstable
world with each region seeking spheres of influence against the other.
What is needed, and has still not been resolved in Europe, is how to harmonise economic efficiency and co-operation without the centralization
of power and the loss of individuality which centralization brings. The
answer, it is suggested, is for Europe to concentrate more on promoting
the aims and purposes of the Council of Europe than the EEC. The two
approaches are inseparable but by placing more emphasis on human
rights and obligations, we may achieve the right balance. Achieving
the right structure of organization between individuals and the state,
and between states and the region, and between regions and on the UN
is of far more importance to world peace and the problems of power
than most people realize.

We have much to learn from the experiences of Switzerland and
Sweden. Both are members of the Council of Europe but neither
are members of the EEC. Both have very prosperous economies
and highly developed democracies. These countries indicate that it is
possible to reconcile the individuality of each nationality within a state
of co-operation to ensure economic success and the protection of human
rights. If this analysis is correct, the future of Europe, and its influence
on the world, should depend on its example of how to harmonize individuality with community, and by its commitments to a wide range of
human rights. Switzerland with its decentralization of power to Canton
level indicates that it is possible to harmonize individuality within a
structure embracing national, regional and international interests. It is

an example which could well be followed by other countries, such as Britain, with devolution of power being given to Scotland and Wales within a wider co-operative concept of national, regional, and international organizations.

Far more progress has been made at the Council of Europe's centre in Strasbourg than most people are aware; something new and exciting is being born there, but like all newly born babies it needs all the loving care politicians can bestow if it is to attain the potential it promises. [2]

Although the motives for providing the huge sum of money to finance the Marshall Plan (over two per cent of the USA's gross national product, i.e. 12,918.8 million US dollars between April 3rd 1948 – June 30th 1952, reported in U.S. State Department Bulletin June 1982) may have been suspect, the fact remains that without that help Western Europe might never have recovered in the way it has. It could so easily have followed the pattern after the First World War when poverty and the deliberate destruction of much of Germany's economy and self-respect as a result of the Versailles Treaty led directly to the Second World War. Massive financial help under the Marshall Plan, following the Second World War, from the USA reversed this approach by injecting the means for economic recovery, but perhaps even more importantly it also injected a spirit of co-operation and goodwill, to provide the political will, without which little could have been accomplished.

Probably the greatest tragedy in today's world is the devaluation of the word 'love'. All the great religions preach its virtues, and the vast majority of people around the world know, in their hearts, that love lies at the heart of all our problems yet all too often we deny it expecting it from others but not from ourselves. If only we as individuals, and as nations, could show more magnanimity and concern for others, without asking for a return, trust and goodwill between individuals and between nations could be assured. All too often we perpetuate a vicious circle of fear by seeking to defend ourselves with more armaments only to find these armaments encourage other nations to do the same.

Nations are not so very different from individuals in their desire to be respected, needing the good opinion of others. Thanks to modern communications international public opinion is now a force in the world, and all politicians take great care to project their best image in

2. See page 114

international conferences and in the media. The potential of this new force has not been appreciated, but, provided we can avoid it being manipulated for propaganda purposes, it could help to dispel myths and promote a greater understanding and knowledge between nations.

UNESCO and the Council of Europe publications, because of their international nature, need all our support and should be encouraged to provide more information and educational material. It is also important to encourage regional international news service by radio and TV, linked when possible to a UN service. So many conflicts are encouraged by misinformation, propaganda and downright lies that an international news service with a reputation for independence and reliability could frequently avert conflict and indirectly encourage respect for law. The Council of Europe is leading the way with many research papers and a splendid assortment of publications with a catalogue of books running into many hundreds of titles.

Lord Franks, who was the Chairman of the Secretariat charged with administering the Marshall Plan made an interesting speech on its 30th anniversary. In this speech he illustrated the manner in which the Organization for European Economic Co-operation limited national sovereignty, when he said:

> The Organization was in permanent session. It possessed a permanent Secretariat which implemented the decisions of the Council and continuously studied the Europe economy. This gave the OEEC an identity of its own. The national delegations, resident in Paris and working closely with the Secretariat, built up an OEEC point of view while keeping their governments fully informed. They, and the Secretariat together devised a number of techniques to persuade governments to a common view. Sir Eric Roll who served with distinction in the British delegation has summed it up: 'The techniques of questionnaire and the mutual analysis of replies, the cross-examination of one's expectations and plans by one's peers, have had a powerful effect in moulding national policies. At the very least they have created a general readiness to 'look over one's shoulder' before taking any major step in foreign policy to ask what the consequences of it might be for one's partners, and how any adverse results might be mitigated. *Subtler in its working, often as powerful, and sometimes even more so, than rigorous constitutional obligations, this habit of consultation and co-operation has resulted in a real limitation of national sovereignty in economic matters*'. (my emphasis)[3]

---

3. Extract taken from *Marshall Plan to Global Interdependence*, an OEEC publication 1978

Since the foregoing was said the Council of Europe has developed a far-reaching interrelated and international complex of parliamentary sessions with committees covering almost every subject. They do not have power but their influence on governments is profound and confirms the observation above. It also confirms my belief in the importance of discovering the right structure of organization.

If the above reasoning is correct then the next step in world affairs must be to encourage more regional grouping with financial help similar to that which enabled the Marshall Plan to be put into operation. The UN is ideally situated to initiate these regional groupings but they will need to be very carefully structured to integrate social, economic and political issues. This is why a chapter is devoted to a Code of Agreement.

If regional groupings are to be established however the principle needs to be established that each nation within the region should owe its first loyalty to the UN. Each individual needs to feel he or she is a world citizen with a loyalty to the local level where local characteristics can be nurtured and expressed in a manner which enriches the cultural needs of the society. Power decentralized in this manner encourages co-operation because small states soon learn to appreciate the benefits of economic co-operation; power decentralized also reduces the possibility of it becoming dangerous and explosive, and gives the individual a greater feeling of belonging. If, as is generally recognised, 'power corrupts and absolute power corrupts absolutely,' then the temptation for the regions to become power blocs with a military capability must be avoided. Decentralization of power would encourage this process and would also help the states within the region to live at peace with each other by encouraging each ethnic, religious and national identity to be expressed in its own cultural manner. Again our task is seen as being that of understanding how to harmonize our opposite needs for individuality with a desire to be wanted and part of the community. This problem of harmonizing apparent opposites in order to create something greater than the separate parts lies at the heart of all our social, economic and political issues and is very relevant to our search for peace.

In international terms, this means the nurturing of small units, each with its own culture but working within an ever widening circle of co-operation. Power must rest, as in all true democracies, with those at the base, with those individuals who are elevated to positions of responsibility using their position to lead and provide good management as the servants of the people not as their masters. This means the end of many people's dream of a UN with power to enforce peace, by violence if need be, under the concept of Collective Security when in reality it can only be secured by consent and through co-operation. This is why the concept of Natural Law and all its implications is so important to understand.

If this approach to peace were to be adopted by the Western nations of Europe, the chances of achieving the dream of a United Europe, including all Eastern Europe, may become a possibility. Already Eastern Germany is seeking a closer association with Western Germany, despite their very different economic philosophies. The door of the Council of Europe should therefore have a 'welcome' sign attached. It should not be impossible to make the original Marshall Plan vision for a united Europe a reality. It will not become a reality however if we always think in terms of defence rather than co-operation. We should encourage all Eastern European countries to join in the work of the Council of Europe in a pragmatic step by step process towards regional peace. It would mean they would have to accept the disciplines of the Council of Europe but this should be possible within their communist philosophy especially if they felt their security was increased. This vision may only become possible if there is also a greater vision of a United Nations encouraging Regional Peace and Development Programmes founded on similar principles in other parts of the world.

If centralized power is to be avoided, the UN must have the capability of enforcing international law to resolve conflicts but must do so without resort to the threat of war, as and when the inevitable conflicts occur.[4] Law must be accepted by consent and cannot be imposed, especially on a state, by acts of violence; on the other hand respect for human rights and the rule of law can be enforced against a government in the same manner as it is enforced in Europe once the social and economic conditions are favourable and the necessary Regional International Courts are established.

The choice is clear: either we conform to the concept of Natural Law or we perish. The old axiom that, 'there can be no freedom except under the law', needs to be broadened to saying, 'there can be no peace except

---

4. This subject is discussed further in the chapter dealing with the UN on page 40

under the law'. This raises the most important question of all as to what constitutes the true basis of law. To answer this question demands a radical change in the popular attitude towards law and order, away from that of law being enforced by violence, to that of law by consent based on our sense of what is fair and just. It means harnessing, through co-operation, the goodwill, trust and confidence of populations; there is no other way as many of those responsible for good policing in national life already recognise.

The nations of the world must encourage and support the generosity of spirit already enshrined in most people's hearts, as was demonstrated in the Bob Geldof campaign for Ethiopia, and the imagination shown by the USA in funding the Marshall Plan. We should then be able to generate sufficient goodwill to proceed step by step, region by region, supporting peace and development programmes, towards the idea of world peace under the law.

The Nature of Law

or Understanding the Relationship between Natural Law, Natural Laws, Law and Regional Peace and Development Programmes

There is considerable confusion about the meaning of, and relationship between, the terms 'Natural Law', 'natural laws' and 'law'. Each has its separate rôle but all are interdependent. When discussing the word 'nature', probably the most important, and obvious, lesson to remember is that health and disease are essential basic requirements for the very existence of the natural world. All living things adapt to their environment: if it is favourable, life will flourish; if unfavourable, disease will gain a foothold and some other form of life more suited to that environment will take its place. If we ignore this fundamental principle of life and attempt to resolve conflict by seeking international agreements which do little to foster a favourable environment encouraging peaceful relationships, the agreements will not bring real peace and the disease of war will sooner or later destroy mankind. If through ignorance or neglect, our social, economic, political and physical environment becomes hostile to human life, then we must not be surprised if we create a sick and violent world such as we are witnessing today with our prisons and mental hospitals full, poverty and famine around the world and war a constant threat. Not only is it necessary to remove the causes of the disease of war, but it is more important positively to promote and nurture healthy international relationships. Thanks to research in the natural sciences we now have sufficient knowledge to create an environment in which we can live in harmony with ourselves and with each other; only when this environment is favourable will our feelings, which dictate our behaviour patterns, respond and generate a climate of opinion in conformity with the basis of Natural Law, a concept fundamental to all law.

The concept of Natural Law is of profound importance and central to all law, yet few subjects have been so neglected, though in recent years a new appreciation of its value is being recognized by international lawyers and philosophers. This has not always been the case. For many centuries there was a universal and intuitive sense of wonder, guided by something beyond our understanding, which many called God and others called Inner Light, Life Force, or Truth. Whatever word is employed nobody denies the presence of the natural world around us. Our task therefore is to understand the nature of the world and the laws governing it and then to translate them into political terms and subsequently into the laws of the land. Failure to co-operate with natural laws can only result in disaster. This is why a clearer understanding of the terms, Natural Law, Natural Laws, and Law is of the utmost importance.

Natural Law

The term Natural Law is an intangible concept which defies any easy definition. It describes a force arising from human conscience and a sense of fairness. It is also a consequence of social, economic and political co-operation. Although the concept has been discussed at length over many centuries, few people agree as to what is exactly meant by the term. Despite this difficulty the idea has profound meaning and importance and cannot be dismissed.

The concept of Natural Law is similar to the idea of Natural Justice, but whereas Natural Justice implies a moral judgement as to what is fair and what is not, Natural Law goes deeper and includes a spiritual dimension based on a recognition of something beyond our understanding such as a 'state of nature' which if recognised will result in a healthy and harmonious society. This 'state of nature' is based on 'life' without which we would all be robots with no sense of meaning or purpose. Unlike law or natural laws, the concept of Natural Law cannot be expressed in scientific or legal terms, even though the philosophers have striven to give it expression over the ages; nevertheless it is constantly referred to by judges in courts of law when making subjective decisions concerning the penalties to be imposed or awards to be made. For instance, we all judge acts by others which affect us by the criteria of fairness and justice; in other words, by the concept of Natural Law. The Oxford Dictionary defines Natural Law as 'based on the innate moral feelings of mankind, instinctively felt to be right and fair'. It is, therefore, a philosophical concept fundamental to our social well-being.

Natural Laws

Natural Laws are easier to understand than the concept of Natural Law because they are capable of being clearly understood as a science. The law of gravity means that the apple always falls from the tree, never upwards; if we eat poison or pollute the earth, we die. Physics and mathematics are subjects which are assumed to help us to make 'progress'. Unfortunately, our understanding is 'through a glass darkly', and frequently, because we cannot see the whole, we make mistakes. Lack of understanding, the attractions of short-term gain at the expense of long-term well-being, or lust for power and prestige, all detract from our willingness or ability to obey and live in harmony with natural laws. Natural laws in themselves do not have the force of law, but indirectly by their logic they compel laws to be enacted by governments; for example, the natural laws of ecology have, in recent years, forced our legislators to address environmental problems as an essential part of government.

The need to study the long-term effects of the natural world, of which man is an integral part, is illustrated by Darwin's study of the earthworm. This study led him to conclude that,

> it may be doubted whether there are many other animals which have played so important a part in the history of the world as have these lowly organized animals. (Faber and Faber 1948 by T.J. Barrett).

This need for a long-term perspective is also dramatised by the experience of Sir Albert Howard, whose famous book *An Agricultural Testament* founded the organic movement. In this book he records a fact which many scientists would say is unbelievable, by claiming, as a result of his experimental, organic compost farming, that he was able to rear oxen on his Indian Agricultural Research Station, without them suffering disease, despite the fact that, 'I have several times seen my oxen rubbing noses with foot and mouth cases. Nothing happened'. (*An Agricultural Testament*. Oxford University Press, 1949.) Despite evidence of this kind no further long term experiments seem to have been undertaken to demonstrate the theory that if the 'Circle of Life' is observed then the healthy phagocytes in the body can overcome the invading germs of disease.

Both Darwin and Howard believed in this 'Circle of Nature', or 'Circle of Life' and that if only we understood the inter-relationship between all the many complex issues involved we could have a healthy environment. Similarly with world affairs we need to understand the nature of a healthy economic, social and political environment. Instead of money determining our future, usually on a short-term basis, we should demand that economics and development conform to the principles involved in the 'Circle of Life'. Laws could then be made to encourage us to practise good husbandry in accordance with the concept of permanency. For instance, a heavy tax could be imposed on the use of nitrogen which would discourage its use and encourage organic farming. Such a tax would also reduce the pollution of our water supplies threatening cancer on a large scale, and simultaneously solve the problems associated with our 'grain mountains', thus releasing several thousand millions of pounds spent subsidising unwanted produce at below cost. The money saved, together with the nitrogen tax, could then be used for promoting a prosperous farming community based on sound agricultural principles.

The search for a healthy world order demands a similar approach to our taxation system; for our wellbeing physically socially and politically. Instead of making our first priority the search for chemicals or medicines to kill disease, or weapons of war to kill our enemies, we should seek to understand the cycle of nature which promotes health, especially a healthy world order. Then we can demand that our politicians promote laws to encourage our farmers, our economies, and our political and international institutions, to conform to sound permanent principles.

The problem is one largely of economics. Many farmers, for instance, would like to become organic growers but are forced for economic reasons to use short-term inorganic methods. This example could be multiplied in almost every industry or technology. Short-term policies also compel nations to adopt economic measures which can only destroy the basic well-being of the country's natural resources.

If the problem is partly economic then we must make economics conform to the natural laws of permanency by tax incentives which encourage good development. Regional Peace and Development Programmes would insist on this approach to development and to the problems of peace by providing the financial resources to help them overcome the difficult period of change.

Law

Law, as usually understood, is the law of the land, as enacted by parliament, to which we either conform or risk being penalized by a court of law. Whether law is good or bad depends on the degree of our understanding about the nature of our spiritual, social and economic environment. If the laws which govern our environment are neglected or deliberately flouted, we pay the penalty. Nature always has the last word. Civilizations in the past have flourished or decayed depending on the philosophy they nurtured. Christianity and other religions provide philosophies which give meaning and purpose to our lives. The need today is for a universal philosophy which all religions and all nations can embrace in our search for world unity with diversity in which each of us can express our personalities within organizations which encourage unity and co-operation; it is not such an impossible notion as may at first appear, once we accept the concept of Natural Law. Law when considered in the above context must be understood in relationship to the concept of Natural Law and the study of natural laws.

Unfortunately, law is generally perceived as being based on coercive powers over others; rule by fear not consent, violence not co-operation. Effective law must depend on trust between the forces of law and the public. If this is destroyed, good law is destroyed. When the law is seen to be violating our sense of fairness, it falls into disrepute. Only when law is seen to be fair and just and in accordance with reason and our environment will it command our support. To ensure that these principles are enforced in accordance with justice and a sense of fairness, a good structure of law administration is vitally important. This means the division of responsibility between those who make the laws, those who make the arrests, and those who adjudicate. If this division is not clearly perceived and understood, then confidence and trust in the process of law will fail and co-operation with those who have the duty to enforce the law turn to hostility.

The Philosophy of Peace and Law

Arguments about the philosophy of peace and law have been continuous since mankind began to formulate concepts of belief. There can be no one definitive philosophy because each of us has different experiences and environmental backgrounds to influence our ideas, but it is essential for us to discover some common ground to help us all to achieve a sense of unity, purpose, and direction. My 'pennyworth' towards finding an answer to this question in relation to international affairs depends on our fundamental beliefs in the nature of life itself and goes as follows:

The most important things in life, such as love, spirit, meaning, and purpose cannot be demonstrated in a scientific manner, yet they are basic to the way we live. We may know the scientific components of life, all its molecules in their minutest detail, but we are still no nearer to knowing the source of life itself. The spirit of man, and all his psychological needs, cannot be dissected on the operating table or traced to source, yet we are quite certain they exist. So although the existence of a Life Force cannot be proved we have plenty of evidence of some Power, or Spirit. The scientist, too, can only express wonder at the unbelievable beauty and complexity of the natural world and the natural laws within which he must conform, learn and obey. The scientist does not make the laws. He explores, seeks to understand, and works in harmony with them. Failure to do so may result in short-term gain but invite long-term disaster.

If the scientific world does not work in accordance with these laws, the result in our national life makes us behave like the motorist driving a very powerful car down a motorway with no sure knowledge of where he is going; with no map, being guided only by short-sighted instincts such as self-interest, power or greed, or just the exhilaration of travelling fast. When he discovers he is travelling in the wrong direction he cannot immediately about-turn but must continue travelling in the same direction from that he knows he should be travelling, in order to arrive at the next junction to enable him to turn and go back.

The fault does not lie only with the scientist but with all of us for supporting the politicians in their blinkered policies. Many scientists are uncomfortably aware of this moral challenge and are refusing to work on projects such as Star Wars and war preparation. The prime responsibility rests with us, the electorate; we must demand from our politicians statesman-like policies which are in accordance with our environment; by their nature these policies are usually long-term requiring us to deny ourselves short-term gains which far too often take us down the fast lane in the wrong direction. Far better to map out the direction we wish to travel and if need be proceed slowly, step by step, region by region, to our destination.

The problem is not an easy one to overcome because our social environment and our self interest encourage us to think and feel in a certain direction. All too often we allow our own desires to reject policies which in other situations we would support. For instance, if we worked in the Sellafield nuclear establishment we would be far more likely to support nuclear power than if we worked somewhere else. Similarly, the richer we become the more likely we are to vote for policies which safeguard our riches, even though those policies may be to the detriment of the country as a whole. Our natural instinct is usually to look for facts and evidence to support something which our own particular situation, or experience, encourages. Subconsciously we look for knowledge and understanding to support policies which are based more on feelings than independent enquiry. We are all susceptible to these pressures and it is necessary for us to recognise their importance so that we may learn to look beyond the immediate future, or short-term gain, and implement policies of a long-term permanent nature.

The cynic may say that to modify man's behaviour patterns by changing his environment is a form of manipulation; but, for better or for worse, we are always manipulating our environment. This is why man is different from the rest of the animal kingdom. Our task is therefore to seek to understand the nature of our social environment which would encourage us to live peacefully together, in harmony with ourselves and others. Mind, spirit and our environment all have a very powerful effect on each other. Our minds have the capacity to comprehend and change the nature of our environment, and the environment has a profound effect on the spirit. This reasoning is important because it affects the manner in which we campaign for change. To demand change, such as unilateral disarmament, by directly challenging governments before a social change has taken place is to put the cart before the horse. If the social and economic environment encourages conflict and war, our first priority must be to campaign for social and economic change.

Our intellect and mind can lead us to recognise the evidence of the Spirit but cannot prove its existence because nobody has yet devised a formula, or method, for isolating it in the test-tube or elsewhere. The evidence however, is so overwhelming that although proof can never be forthcoming it takes but a small step to believe in a power beyond ourselves, a power which works through nature, including us as individuals. Evidence in the natural world shows that if we work in harmony with natural laws, the probability of creating beauty, life and peace is enhanced. If we fail to respect nature, disease, ugliness and conflict must result.

There is also evidence of people's lives being transformed through a spiritual experience, enabling them to live in harmony with their environment, sometimes even when all the odds are stacked against them. Looking for the good in others and reaching out to them in a spirit of generosity can also transform enmity into friendship. The spirit of the age may be for good or evil purposes. The Marshall Plan inspired a spirit of co-operation after the Second World War and led to peace. By way of contrast, the heavy burden of reparations imposed on Germany by the vindictive Versailles Treaty after the First World War created feelings of injustice and led directly to war in 1939.

Justice, inspired by concern for the good of others, encourages good relationships. For instance, we all want justice as a natural right and react strongly against all injustice, especially if it affects us personally. Conscience and a moral code recognise right from wrong and we also recognise the rights of a court of justice to inflict punishment, provided that the punishment fits the crime and does not offend against natural justice and is curative in its treatment of the offender. The concept of justice is generally recognised as the basic requirement for all law but unless it is tempered with mercy it will fail. Portia in *The Merchant of Venice* demonstrated this when Shylock demanded his pound of flesh. Justice without compassion can be cruel and provoke rebellion, and what seems to be justice may appear as injustice, as many conflicts in the world testify. Vague pleadings for love and truth therefore need to be translated into more meaningful political terms or they will be dismissed as unrealistic woolly idealism.

This is why the concept of justice is so important; justice can be formulated legally and applied in courts of law. It has been translated into many forms such as Magna Carta, and the UN Universal Declaration of Human Rights. Conventions of all kinds have also agreed to implement these Rights but this process has only just begun and urgently needs more support; Regional Peace and Development Programmes would encourage this process. It should be stressed, however, that the objective is not to encourage more law *per se*, but to encourage an environment supported by law to enable individuals to live a freer life without the law. In other words, to encourage them to learn to live a life which respects the freedoms of others.

Closely allied to the ideas of love, truth and justice are the ideas of trust and confidence without which there can be no effective international agreements. When trust and confidence break down, suspicion of motives increases and the seeds of conflict are sown. For those sceptics who doubt the strength of moral power we have the examples of Gandhi liberating India, and Martin Luther King liberating the blacks in the USA. The liberating power of truth in the form of knowledge and information is also shown by the inability of the British, Dutch and French to retain their hold on their empires, even for small colonies such as Aden, once subject peoples become aware, through TV and radio, of their human rights. All the armies of these colonial powers were unable to prevent the dissolution of their empires; a phenomenon totally unrecognised by most people yet of profound importance if we are to understand how to mobilise public opinion against war. Ignorance is the ally of the oppressor, but knowledge, truth and access to information have made the modern world a very different place.

Military force cannot suppress rebellions for long once the liberating power of the spirit has been awakened to freedom and equality. When military power seeks to impose its will on a people nursing grievances resulting from injustices it invariably digs its own grave if it becomes involved in a military exercise involving killing innocent people. Military action by its nature kills indiscriminately and consequently increases fear and hatred, perpetuating injustice and conflict. Military power cannot win the hearts and minds of people; quite the opposite.

Gandhi and King both understood, and harnessed, the power of truth in their struggles for freedom, and through the media they spoke truth to Power. Moral power, as Gandhi, King and Jesus taught us, demands that we be patient, quiet and listen to the promptings of truth and conscience. Similarly, development programmes need long and careful preparation and should not be implemented until there has been patient observation over a long period of the needs of the people involved. Instant answers based on an alien technology may only 'pave the way to hell with good intentions', as many inappropriate development programmes have proved. On the other hand, if environmental development programmes are introduced to the regions of the world, founded on the concepts of permanence and self-reliance, the reasons for war are reduced and the basis for law encouraged. Regional Peace and Development Programmes should seek to encourage this process.

The power of truth could be even more effective today as a means of preventing conflict. At present, each nation has its own point of view to present to its own people and to the world, and invariably that point of view is biased, especially when disputes between nations arise. Each nation of course has the right to present its own point of view, but far more emphasis should be given to regional and international organs for assembling and disseminating knowledge, information and news. This process has already begun, and UNESCO and the Council of Europe are performing valuable work through their conferences and journals, such as the *Courier* and *Development Forum* and the embryo UN radio and UN University. The Council of Europe also has the excellent journal called *Forum* and a wide range of other material. All these activities have laid down good foundations for future development but they represent only the beginning of what should become the natural means by which everyone can gain access to reliable, independent news and information. International understanding should be one of our first priorities if international law is to become a reality and the causes of war removed. That the power of truth is recognised by governments is shown by the manner they suppress truth whenever they feel threatened. In many instances it is doubtful if governments could obtain the people's assent to wage war if they allowed the public to know all the facts in an unbiased manner. Regional Peace and Development programmes would encourage regional sources of knowledge and information similar to those which the Council of Europe is beginning to provide.

Jesus lived, taught, and practised by the power of the spirit, healing both the spiritual and physical ailments of man. We also know from our own experience the need to live in harmony with the spirit within each of us and between all of us. Unfortunately our social environment all too often denies us the opportunities for self-expression and for feeling part of the community; consequently the spirit within us turns sour and seeks expression by committing anti-social acts, including acts of violence so commonly seen today. Regional programmes would encourage a favourable community spirit of co-operation and thus remove the causes of disruption.

The spirit by which we live is also enhanced by the sense of wonder we all experience when we gaze at the universe and appreciate its limitless space, or study the minutest atom. These amazing wonders of the natural world compel our admiration and test our comprehension. This admiration is increased by the realisation that Nature demands a delicate and integrated system of order and balance; failure to comply with natural laws will result in disease and death. Thus, because man is an animal, we are an integral part of that complex kingdom and must discover the laws of Nature if we are to live in harmony with her.

Mankind is only just beginning to discover the frontiers of the spirit, which, understood better, might help us to create an environment where individuals would find meaning, purpose and satisfaction. If we devoted as much attention to understanding the natural laws of the spirit as we do to the natural laws of physics, the world would not be in the chaotic state it is today.

Nature, however, is composed of such opposites as night and day with each a complementary part of the other, and therefore our task is to understand how these opposites can be harmonized to create something greater than either alone can attain. Nowhere is this seen more clearly than in international relationships. As individuals, we all need space and freedom to express our individuality, but at the same time we need to feel part of a group with a local identity, a group with whom we can share our loyalty and express our personality through work and play in the community. The study of animal behaviour shows that if the personality and individuality of animals are not respected, conflict occurs. This usually means the provision of sufficient territory in which the animals can breed, rear families and find self-expression.

The need for individuality and community is also a basic require-ment for man. Dr. Schumacher identified this need for individuality and self-expression with his splendid idea of 'small is beautiful'. This concept, however, neglected to point out that small is also vulnerable and needs protection from more powerful neighbours. I therefore see the co-operation of small units as essential for political freedoms and survival. Co-operation should prove easier for small states because only through a system of co-operation can their security be assured. Regional Peace and Development Programmes could ensure this mixture of local loyalties within a regional system of co-operation.

Our need for individuality and community is often portrayed, in political terms, as either capitalist or socialist, when in reality both ideologies contain the germ of something essential to our human requirements. Our task is to harmonise these apparent opposites into something greater than either alone can attain. The harmonization of apparent opposites is a common feature in nature, the understanding of which involves many disciplines. Judged solely on a narrow, selfish point of view, therefore, our task is to discover new forms of international co-operation in which each state can find peace, security and well-being through mutual aid, first, through regional organizations, and eventually through a world organization such as the UN. The individuality of the person needs to be nurtured in small units at a very local level, within larger and larger groupings until global co-operation is achieved, but always under a system of law which respects individual human rights.

The idea of small units co-operating within a region has also been found to be a sound management principle in commerce and in most walks of life. Trees illustrate this principle, with each leaf expressing its own individuality, obtaining nourishment through its many branches but from one central source. Ecology illustrates the interdependence of all life, with each part having an identity of its own which must be cherished if the whole is to be preserved and enhanced.

The principle of unity with diversity is summed up in the old Quaker saying, 'In essentials, unity; in non-essentials, liberty; in all things, love'. This idea was expressed in a different form by Jesus when he said that the first commandment is to love God and the second to love your neighbour, and that everything else flows from these two commandments. Gandhi also made a valuable contribution along similar lines when he coined the idea of Satyagraha, or Truth Force, in which he equated the idea of God with Truth, believing that Truth, if obeyed, has a moral force of its own stronger than violence. These teachings are fundamentally simple in concept, being based on truth, reason and conscience. Unfortunately these essentials are usually dismissed in the political world without serious consideration and violent solutions substituted. If they were realised we could have world unity between all religions and all faiths. All religions profess to believe in the ideal of love, while atheists and agnostics, if not accepting the concept of God, nevertheless respect the need to conform to natural laws for the social well-being of mankind. Considered in this context we could have a unifying ideology for world peace within the UN. Many UN conferences already prove the viability of this approach; for example, the conference on the problems of pollution in the Mediterranean depended on the co-operation of all the nations in the area, irrespective of race or religion, in pursuance of a common aim.

To reach for a world of perfect peace, however, in which there are no conflicts is not only unrealistic but undesirable because conflict is an inherent part of human nature without which there cannot be progress. Without struggle and a degree of conflict the world would be sterile and meaningless; but if we can discover a unity of purpose alongside our diversities, as outlined above, whenever the fundamental rights of man are violated, law could be enforced, not by violence but by moral forces upheld by social and economic justice; the potentialities of which we have barely begun to appreciate. Gandhi harnessed world opinion behind the concept of 'truth force' and won freedom for India, and Martin Luther King won liberation from oppression in the USA for the blacks. Regional Peace and Development Programmes could do the same for the regions of the world and liberate them from fear of poverty and war.

Appendix

George Marshall's Speech at Harvard University

This historic address, which initiated the Marshall Plan, was made by Secretary of State George C. Marshall to Harvard University on June 5th 1947. After the first half of Marshall's address, in which he outlined the manner by which the European economy had collapsed, he continued:

The modern system of the division of labour upon which the exchange of products is based is in danger of collapse. The truth of the matter is that Europe's requirements for the next three or four years of foreign food and other essential products—principally from America—are so much greater than her present ability to pay that she must have substantial additional help or face economic, social and political deterioration of a very grave character.

The remedy lies in breaking the vicious circle and restoring the confidence of the European people in the economic future of their own countries and of Europe as a whole. The manufacturer and the farmer throughout wide areas must be able and willing to exchange their product for currencies the continuing value of which is not open to question.

Aside from the demoralizing effect on the world at large and the possibilities of disturbances arising as a result of the desperation of the people concerned, the consequences to the economy of the United States should be apparent to all. It is logical that the United States should do whatever it is able to do to assist in the return of normal economic health in the world, without which there can be no political stability and no assured peace. Our policy is not against any country or doctrine but against hunger, poverty, desperation, and chaos. Its purpose should be the revival of a working economy in the world so as to permit the emergence of political and social conditions in which free institutions can exist. Such assistance, I am convinced, must not be on a piecemeal basis as various crises develop. Any assistance that this government may render in the future should provide a cure rather than a mere palliative...

It is already evident that, before the United States government can proceed much further in its efforts to alleviate the situation and help start the European world on its way to recovery, there must be some agreement amongst the countries of Europe as to the requirements of the situation and the part those countries themselves will take in order to give proper effect to whatever action might be undertaken by this government. It would be neither fitting nor efficacious for this Government to undertake to draw up unilaterally a program designed to place Europe on its feet economically. That is the business of the Europeans. The initiative, I think, must come from Europe. The role of this country should consist of friendly aid in the drafting of a European program and of later support of such a program as far as it is practical for us to do so. The program should be a joint one, agreed to by a number, if not all, European nations.

An essential part of any successful action on the part of the United States is an understanding on the part of the people of America of the character of the problem and the remedies to be applied. Political passion and prejudice should have no part. With foresight, and a willingness on the part of our people to face up to the vast responsibility which history has clearly placed on our country, the difficulties I have outlined can and will be overcome.

This address appeared in the book *From Marshall Plan to Global Interdependence*, alongside other addresses made at a Commemorative Dinner given by the Secretary-General of the Organization for Economic Co-operation and Development. Published 1978 and available from the OECD office in Paris. £8.50.

Commenting on the Above Speech, Roy Jenkins in his book *Truman* (Collins 1986. £2.95) writes:

Marshall also took three key decisions himself. The first was that speed was essential. Otherwise Europe might disintegrate in front of benevolent but too leisurely eyes. 'The patient is sinking while the doctors deliberate,' he said. The second was that Europe get together and produce a plan for its own recovery. The United States would then do its best to produce what was needed to sustain the plan. But it must not produce both the supplies and the plan; or at least not be seen to do so. Third, and most controversially, he decided that the offer must be made to Europe as a whole and not to the non-Communist part of it.

Lord Lever and Christopher Huhne Commenting on How Marshall Aid Helped Europe

Lord Lever of Manchester (Harold Lever) and Christopher Huhne in their Penguin book *Debt and Danger* (1985) after discussing how international co-operation includes positive transfers to poorer nations, continue:

> The clearest example of this was the large programme of financial flows to Europe after the Second World War to aid its reconstruction. The lessons of German reparations after the First World War had been learned. Between 1949 and 1952 the United States transferred the equivalent of 4.5 per cent of its GNP in Marshall Aid, the largest instance of sustained international financial flows in history. Yet far from reducing the USA's level of National income, even a cursory glance at its national accounts shows an acceleration of growth and of personal incomes during that period. The Marshall Plan was certainly generous, but it involved an enlightened and self-interested generosity; as a result, the USA once again had a trading partner and competitor which ensured both that the level of world trade was given a substantial fillip and that there were positive welfare gains through greater choice and competition. Both Europe and the USA benefited.

Lord Lever was successively the financial adviser to the British Prime Ministers Harold Wilson and James Callaghan and a member of their respective cabinets. He was also chairman of a group of financial experts asked by the Commonwealth Prime Ministers to report on the debt crisis which they did in 1984 in a publication entitled *Debt Crisis and the World Economy*.

Christopher Huhne broadcaster and writer is the economics editor of the *Guardian* for which he writes a weekly column.

The Marshall Plan by Barbara Ward

An extract from an article in *Foreign Affairs* called 'Another Chance for the North?' (written in support of the Brandt Report), taken from the *American Quarterly Review* 1980/81.

> The whole boom of the 1950s and 1960s would have been inconceivable without the launching of the Marshall Plan which in giving away over five years a goodly two per cent of a much poorer America's GNP ensured its own prosperity along with that of its neighbours in the North.
>
> The memory of the Marshall Plan is a reminder of one last point. True the Plan was in part fuelled by the Cold War just as today limits to Soviet

adventurism could reasonably be evoked for the Brandt proposals. But another element was quite simply compassion—ordinary Americans feeling the good fortune of surviving so appalling a holocaust and ready to share with fellow survivors the means of rebuilding their lives. Is this feeling of compassionate responsibility entirely dead in the North?

The Marshall Plan

Extract from a *Guardian* editorial of February 24th 1987 headed 'Solving Brazil's Debt Crisis'

> What is needed is nothing less than a new Marshall Plan. At the moment debtors are getting neither concerted financial help nor the hope of faster world growth to boost their export earnings. The Baker Plan to pump more banking money into debtor countries never got off the ground. The weekend meeting of the Group of Five produced nothing to commit either Japan or West Germany to expand their economies by more than they were already planning. A Marshall Plan would recognise that the reality of the matter is that some of the Third World's debts must be written down and rescheduled and that financial supply lines from the industrial countries must be re-opened. And that this should take place against a back-ground of faster world growth. The pivotal role in all this should be played by Japan which is sitting on top of $92 billion trade surplus. If something like this does not happen the West must not be surprised if defaulting becomes the norm rather than the exception.

How About a Marshall Plan for the Mexicans?

An extract from an article by Dr. Stephany Griffith-Jones (a teacher at the Institute of Development Studies, University of Sussex), 'on a visionary but modest proposal'. Printed in the *Guardian*, 9th October 1985.

After discussing the debt crisis facing Mexico Dr. Stephany Griffith-Jones continues:

> I wonder whether the Mexican earthquake could not provide the spark—or the excuse—for significantly increased official flows, first to Mexico and then to other Latin American countries. If out of the rubble of a destroyed Europe emerged the idealistic and economically tremendously successful Marshall Plan, could not a more modest—though equally visionary—programme emerge from the rubble of Mexico City?

105

Keynes Revisited...and a Marshall Plan for the Third World

Below are extracts from an article by a former governor of
the National Bank of Greece, Professor A. Angelopoulos. From
Development Forum Nov/Dec 1986.

The inability of developing countries to repay their external debt, now
amounting to at least $1000 billion, with an annual service (interest and
amortization) of about $150 billion, may provoke the collapse of both
the banking and financial systems and a new world crisis of gigantic
dimensions......

In two recent studies, I have made proposals to avoid a general
crisis of the international banking system and to revive world economic
growth. (*Global Plan for Economic Growth. A New Marshall Plan.*
Praeger Publishers, New York 1983). The first proposal envisages an
immediate approach to the existing debt problem—rearrangement of
the existing debts to private banks—and the second, a new government
funded long-term financial system......

The plan proposed above is based on the application of a Keynesian
policy on an international scale. It is a principal thesis of my book,
mentioned above, that under present conditions, Keynesian theory can no
longer be effective when applied only on a national scale, for economic,
social, technical and other reasons. But if applied on an international
scale its objectives could be achieved. We have to adopt towards the
poor countries the same policy that was applied successfully by the
industrialized countries towards their lower-income populations. That
policy ensured full employment and sustained economic growth for a
quarter of a century.

Contadora's New Peace Search
Report in the *Guardian* of September 8th 1983.

The seventh attempt at getting nine regional countries to agree on
a formula for a peaceful end to Central American conflicts began
here yesterday.

The four foreign ministers of the Contadora group—Mexico,
Columbia, Venezuela, and Panama—met in preliminary talks before
joining five Central American foreign ministers in full session.

Their last full conference collapsed amid Nicaraguan charges that
US allies in Central America were sabotaging peace efforts. Honduras,
Costa Rica, Guatemala, and El Salvador stood together in opposition to
Nicaragua which is accused by Washington of trying to export a Marxist
revolution throughout the region.........

The group is using a plan drawn up by the Contadora presidents in
July to try and force a peace proposal acceptable to all nine countries.

The key points call for an end to foreign military advisers and bases in the region and a halt to arms trafficking.

Washington claims that Nicaragua supplies guerrillas in El Salvador with arms and support. Salvadorean guerrillas have fought back the US-backed army there for nearly four years.

Extracts from the Commonwealth Heads of Government Meeting in Nassau October 1985 Supporting Regional Initiatives

para. 11. Heads of Government welcomed the wide range of approaches suggested in the Group's Report directed at enabling small states to become more self-reliant both through their own initiatives and through bilateral and multilateral action. They also endorsed the Report's emphasis on the increased potential for action at the regional level.

para. 12....They stressed too the relevance of support for regional efforts to help overcome the problems emanating from small size.

para. 32. Heads of Government expressed their belief that nuclear weapon free zones, on the basis, among other criteria, of agreements freely arrived at among states of a region, could constitute an important disarmament measure. They welcomed the adoption of the South Pacific Nuclear Free Zone Treaty by the South Pacific Forum on August 6th 1985 at Raratonga as an important step in global and regional efforts to prevent nuclear proliferation.

para. 35. They also agreed on the need for a comprehensive political settlement (in Kampuchea) which would ensure peace in the region....

para. 36. As a further means of ensuring lasting peace and stability in the region (S.E. Asia), Heads of Government noted with approval efforts being made towards the early establishment of a zone of peace, freedom and neutrality in the region and urged all states to fully support these efforts.

para. 37. Heads of Government noted with satisfaction the reduction of tension in the area, and the efforts to strengthen regional co-operation in the Caribbean and pledged their support for the region's collective efforts to accelerate development.

para. 38. ...they expressed continuing support for the Contadora Group's efforts to promote dialogue with the aim of finding lasting solutions to the region's problems and promoting its development.

Letter from the Directorate-General for Development of the Commission of the European Communities (EEC) in response to the suggestion that the EC should support the Proposal for Regional Peace and Development Programmes

27th March 1987

Dear Sir,

Thank you for your interest shown and your suggestion for the negotiations of the next Convention between the European Community and the ACP (African, Caribbean and Pacific) countries. We entirely share your opinion concerning the importance of special support for regional development. Therefore we have dedicated Title V11 of the Third Lomé Convention to 'regional co-operation' in order to strengthen the ACP States' collective capabilities. The Convention says that 'the Community shall provide effective aid to achieve the objectives and priorities which have set themselves in the context of regional co-operation.'

Since the beginning of the Lomé policy in 19875 funds have been reserved for regional co-operation projects. In fact 1 billion ECU out of a total amount of 8.5 billion ECU being made available to the APC States under the Third Lomé Convention is specifically earmarked for such projects and programmes. There is good reason to believe that 'regional co-operation' will remain a subject of major concern in the future.

Yours sincerely

F. Nicora
Head of Division

Calls for an International Criminal Court

The following article by Anna Tomforde in the *Guardian* of November 25th 1985 was headed 'Nuremberg Call for Rights Court':

An international lawyers' conference examining the contemporary relevance of the Nuremberg War Crimes Tribunal heard calls at the weekend for the creation of an international court to deal with human rights offences such as those in Kampuchea and Uganda, equated apartheid with Nazi-ism and demanded a 'magna carta' for the nuclear age.

The meeting called by the International Association of Democratic Lawyers, was to mark the fortieth anniversary of the trial of 21 ringleaders of the Nazi regime by the victorious Allied powers. The 400 representatives of the legal profession from 13 West European and Eastern bloc countries agreed that the principles of Nuremberg were still valid and should be developed into universal jurisdiction banning crimes against humanity.

The former deputy US prosecutor at the trial, Professor Robert Kempner spoke for the overwhelming majority of participants when he dismissed criticism that the Nuremberg trial had no basis in law and that it constituted the imposition of the law of the victor on the vanquished.

'Those who are against Nuremberg today are those who want war, ex-friends or successors of the war criminals or right wing extremists', the 87-year-old professor said.

Anna Tomforde's article continues by reporting Lord Gifford Q.C. as saying:

'This conference must not simply be a pious commemoration of a past event of 1945. It must be the occasion for examining the responsibility of the leaders of 1985 for the perpetration in 1985 of similar international crimes.'

He (Lord Gifford) singled out the Apartheid regime in South Africa which he referred to as 'the Nazism of our time' as the most conspicuous example of crimes against humanity and 'aggressive war' today.

Lord Gifford and others called for the establishment of an international tribunal even if only equipped with moral authority before which today's political leaders could be held accountable.

The call was endorsed by Mr. Anthony Marreco, a member of the British legal team at the Nuremberg trials, who said that a 'permanent Nuremberg' was needed in the form of an international court to deal with present-day violations of human rights in countries such as Kampuchea and Uganda. 'Failing that, (he continued) we need to develop universal jurisdiction and an international statute for crimes that would incorporate the 1948 Genocide Prevention Act and the new Torture Convention and the Geneva Convention.'

Iran: Case for an International Criminal Law

by Peter Archer Q.C., Solicitor-General to the last Labour Government.

The extract below is taken from an article with the above title in the *Guardian* May 5th 1980.

The Iranian students who are detaining American citizens have undoubtedly infringed Iranian criminal law but clearly no proceedings will be brought against them by the Iranian authorities. International pressure on the Iranian government urging it to comply with its obligations has met with little response. This may be the occasion to review proposals for an international criminal law with its own international court. For the present, at least, it would have to rely for its sanctions upon the police forces and the prison systems of individual states. But all civilised states would bind themselves to apprehend and hand over for trial anyone suspected of an offence wherever he may be found. And nationals of any state which refused to enforce the jurisdiction would know that, if they infringed the provisions, they would never be able to set foot outside its borders without inviting arrest and trial.

This is by no means the first time that the problem has arisen. It has manifested itself in connection with terrorists and highjackers. And in order to ensure that Eichmann was tried for crimes committed in Germany, Israeli agents were compelled to abduct him unlawfully from Argentina. Yet it is apparent that unless governments cease to offer sanctuary to those, whether at home or abroad, who have committed wrongs against nationals of other states, the world will be a jungle, where no one is safe.

Proposal for a UN High Commissioner for Human Rights

by Sean MacBride, eminent international jurist. President of the Committee of Ministers of the Council of Europe.

Extract taken from the chapter *Human Rights and the Rule of Law* by Sean MacBride in the symposium *Foundations of Peace and Freedom* (See page 123)

Independently of any international judicial machinery for the protection of human rights, there is a vitally important proposal before the United Nations for the establishment of a *United Nations High Commissioner for Human Rights* with a status somewhat analogous to the High Commissioner for Refugees. When established, this institution will provide the UN with a modest but useful instrument for the fulfilment of its mandate under Article 13 (1) of the Charter, to assist 'in the realization of human rights and fundamental freedoms for all'. The High Commissioner for Human Rights is not intended to form part of the machinery for the implementation, of existing or future international instruments relating to human rights, he is rather intended to be complementary to such machinery. He will have power to give advice and assistance to the United Nations organs which request it, and will be of considerable value to bodies such as the Commission on Human Rights which is not organised in such a way as to enable it to undertake detailed examination of particular problems and has no independent authority to which it could entrust such a task. The High Commissioner for Human Rights could also render assistance to governments in regard to problems affecting human rights when requested to do so, and through his report to the General Assembly, he could play an important part in encouraging the better protection of human rights at all levels and in securing the ratification of international conventions relating to human rights.

The proposal for the institution of a High Commissioner for Human Rights is most worthy of the support of those anxious to promote the cause of human rights. It would make a useful contribution to the protection of human rights which would be acceptable to a large majority of member states of the United Nations, since in no way can it be said to encroach on their national sovereignty and while providing them with an institution to which they may turn for assistance, refrains from any unsolicited interference in their domestic affairs.

Extract from Letter from the Foreign and Commonwealth Office by Evan Luard

written while acting as Parliamentary Under-Secretary of State on the 24th October 1977 in support of the proposal for a United Nations High Commissioner for Human Rights.

...I very much agree with what Mr. MacBride said about the post of High Commissioner. We have actively pressed for the establishment of such a post for some years. When the hostility of Eastern European countries and lack of enthusiasm on the part of the non-aligned countries prevented useful progress being made in the General Assembly, we sponsored Resolution 3221 in an attempt to broaden discussion. It has always been our policy to keep the idea of a High Commissioner in the forefront of attention, and we welcomed President Carter's support for the idea in his speech at the United Nations on March 17th.

The General Assembly will be debating in the near future the agenda item to which Resolution 3221 relates. Mr. Dunn will be interested to know that the United Kingdom is one of a small group of countries engaged in a careful but determined effort to revive the proposal for a High Commissioner. Intensive lobbying preparatory to debate is now in progress. I return your constituent's letter.

Yours sincerely,

Evan Luard.

(The above extract was sent to me in response to my letter enclosing a copy of Mr. MacBride's article on page 110). In view of the changed attitude by the Soviet government in recent months (1987) the time is opportune to revive this proposal.

Nuremberg: Greatest Trial in History

Extract from an article written by Airey Neave, Conservative MP. who was later killed in his car by the IRA outside the House of Commons. *The Observer* November 5th 1978.

After arguing that the Nuremberg Trial was necessary and better than simply putting Goering and the others up against a wall and shooting them, Airey Neave adds:

> It can be claimed that Nuremberg, by excluding the defence of 'superior orders' has influenced the laws of war and defined the responsibilities of soldiers. American and British military manuals now declare that a soldier is only obliged to obey 'lawful orders'. No order is to be carried out by the Army of the Federal Republic of Germany if it would lead to a crime.

The Nuremberg Principles by Seán MacBride

Eminent international jurist, president of the Committee of Ministers of the Council of Europe 1949−50.

The abstract below is taken from Séan MacBride's chapter 'Human Rights and the Rule of Law' in *Foundations of Peace and Freedom*.

> It is, however, time that *criminal* sanctions for acts of war, aggression and brutality were applied to individuals, and that a permanent international criminal tribunal were established for this purpose. A bold new concept of international jurisdiction was adopted under the Charter of the International Military Tribunal which dealt with war crimes at the end of the Second World War. This jurisdiction affirmed, 'the existence of fundamental human rights superior to the law of the state and protected by international criminal sanctions even if violated in pursuance of the law of the State'. (G.A. Resolution 177 (11) para(a).) The one major defect was that this was jurisdiction to try the vanquished by the victors. Nevertheless it reflected a universal reaction against the atrocities committed before and during the war, and a determination to punish those guilty of such atrocities. Later, in 1950, the principles on which the jurisdiction was based were confirmed in the *Nuremberg Principles* formulated by the International Law Commission following a directive of the General Assembly of the United Nations.
>
> The *Principles* constitute highly authoritative guides as to the character of the legal obligations of citizens and leaders in regard to war crimes, crimes against humanity and crimes against peace; *they place criminal responsibility on individuals for the commission of any of the crimes defined.*
>
> Principle 1 which provides that, 'any person who commits an act which constitutes a crime under international law is responsible therefore and liable to punishment' emphasizes that international law may impose duties directly on individuals. Moreover, the fact that the internal law of a country does not impose a penalty for an act which

constitutes a crime under international law does not relieve the person who commits the act from responsibility under international law (Principle 11). Superior orders do not relieve the person who commits the act from his responsibility, provided that a moral choice was in fact possible (Principle 1V). The Nuremberg Tribunal has declared that killings or torture under orders in violation of the international law of war had never been recognized as a defence for such acts of brutality, although the order of the superior could be urged in mitigation of punishment.

The crimes punishable under international law were defined by the International Law Commission under three headings in Principle V1, ...crimes against peace, war crimes, and crimes against humanity (Detailed in *Foundations of Peace and Freedom*). In its definition of crimes against humanity the Commission omitted the phrase 'before or during the war' contained in Article 6 (c) of the Charter of the Nuremberg Tribunal, because this phrase referred to the particular war of 1939. The omission reflects the opinion of the Commission that crimes against humanity may take place even before a war in connection with crimes against peace.

Criminal responsibility is placed on both governments and individuals by the Genocide Convention of 1948. Article 4 provides:

'persons committing genocide, or any other of the acts defined in Article 3, shall be punished, whether they are constitutionally responsible rulers, public officials or private individuals.'

It emerges clearly from these developments that there should be established a permanent international tribunal to deal with all crimes defined in the Hague and Geneva Conventions, the Nuremberg Principles and the Genocide Convention. Such a permanent judicial tribunal would not suffer from the defect of being set up on an ad hoc basis to deal with a particular situation. Its decisions might remain temporarily unenforceable in some regions, but the individual offender could at least be identified and branded as an outlaw. Such a sanction would have a restraining influence and would reduce the trend towards the brutalisation of mankind.

A further aspect of this new approach to the right to wage war is the individual's right to refuse to participate in a war, which derives logically from the criminal liability described above. The combined effect of Articles 6 and 8 of the Charter of the International Military Tribunal was to make every soldier liable for crimes against peace, war crimes, and crimes against humanity. The fact that he was acting 'pursuant to the order of his Government, or his superior, shall not free him from responsibility'. This liability having been confirmed by the Nuremberg Principles each individual therefore must make a value judgement before participating in any war, or obeying certain military orders if he is not to incur the risk of becoming a war criminal. The question of *refusing* military service and orders is thus no longer a question of pure conscience (the classic conception of 'conscientious objection'); it is also in many cases a legal obligation under international law.

The Council of Europe

The Council of Europe's work is often overshadowed and confused with the work of the European Community (the Organization for Economic Co-operation and Development). The European Community is primarily concerned with economic co-operation, while the Council of Europe works, to quote from the official Guide to the Council. (*The Council of Europe 1986*).

> to improve the lives of Europeans through practical, often unspectacular action in a very wide range of fields, as this booklet shows. It does this through organizing co-operation between the governments of its member states. But this is not enough: Europe is not limited to governments, parliaments and other institutions. Real European unity depends on the will, the understanding and the active participation of millions of individuals who make up the continent. This is the guiding principle of the Council of Europe.

In 1943 Churchill first expressed the idea that regional councils would be required to deal with the problems facing the world after the war, but it was not until May 1949 that the Council of Europe was set up following the commencement of the Marshall Plan which was launched on June 5th 1947. The Treaty of Rome which initiated the EC was signed later in 1957.

The EC member states number only 11, while the Council of Europe numbers 21 including states such as Switzerland, Norway and Sweden who are not members of the EC.

Though the Council's work is largely carried out through inter-governmental co-operation, the interests of the individual remain its prime concern.

The aims of the Council of Europe are:

a. To work for the greater European Unity.
b. To uphold the principles of parliamentary democracy, the rule of law and human rights.
c. To improve living conditions and promote human values.

The Council's Statute declares that each member state must recognize the principle of the rule of law and guarantee its citizens the enjoyment of human rights and fundamental freedoms. Any European state that accepts these democratic principles can apply to become a member. Since 1949 the membership has grown from 10 to 21 countries representing practically the whole of non-communist Europe.

Its Structure consists of a Committee of Ministers, and an Assembly composed of national members of parliaments and involves local authorities and non-governmental organizations in its deliberations.

In Scope the Council covers practically all aspects of European affairs with the exception of defence.

In Membership the Council includes all the European Community states, a number of 'neutral' and 'non-aligned' countries and other European democracies who share its ideals. It also opens many of its activities to non-member states, thus extending co-operation beyond the 21. It is this combination of wide membership, general competence and a flexible structure that gives the Council of Europe its unique character.

The Conscience of Europe

by Lord Carrington, PC, KCMG, MC, when UK Secretary of State for Foreign and Commonwealth Affairs
Chairman-in-office of the Committee of Ministers of the Council of Europe. January 1982.

Extract from an article in *Forum* 1/82, the Council of Europe's official quarterly journal.

> Many people may not realize the extent to which the decisions of the Court and Commission of Human Rights in Strasbourg can influence United Kingdom legislation and practice.
> The Council of Europe is, with every justification, renowned for its role as the conscience of Europe through its work on human rights. Its Convention on Human Rights continues to be the only international instrument for the protection of Human Rights which is backed up by effective judicial machinery, and which has repeatedly demonstrated that effectiveness in practice.

South Africa after Apartheid

The book *After Apartheid: The Solution*, reviewed below, corresponds closely with the aims of the proposal for Regional Peace and Development Programmes. It was reviewed by the Institute of Social Inventions in *The Guardian* of March 18th 1987.

This month in South Africa, a group called Groundswell formally adopts its constitution. With prominent members of the business community as trustees, it aims to promote the ideas in *After Apartheid: The Solution* (£8 from the Alternative Bookshop 3, Langley Court London WC2). This book has an enthusiastic foreword by Winnie Mandela and in the Africaner edition an endorsement from the government's Transport Minister.

Its authors, Leon Louw and Frances Kendall, set out how South Africa could be cantonised along Swiss lines with decision-making decentralised initially to the present magisterial districts (which have an average population of 80,000 each). This would lead to the formation of some 100 cantons within a national confederation, with an unconditional universal franchise. Additional safeguards would be a Bill of Rights to protect minorities, the abolition of governmental apartheid, complete freedom of movement between cantons and, by referendum, the right of a canton to secede from the confederation (or to be expelled).

The authors of the above are due to make a presentation of their ideas to the ANC in Lusaka. Already they have been warmly received by left and right, ranging from white nationalists to former oppostion leader Frederick van Zyl Slabbert and Chief Buthelezi. The book has been top of the non-fiction best seller lists. In her foreword to the latest edition, Winnie Mandela writes, 'an excellent historical alternative all freedom lovers will embrace'.

Reform of UN—An Internal UN Watchdog Report

Extracts from a *Guardian* article September 30th 1986 by Hanns Neuerboiurg in Geneva:

An internal UN Watchdog Report released this morning says that the United Nations system is beset with numerous 'unacceptable' shortcomings and calls for radical structural reforms.

The Report analyses the fragmentation of available resources, poor co-ordination, mediocre outputs, insufficient staff qualification, and overlapping jurisdictions between various UN organs which have created a 'state of confusion'.

It (the Report) says that reforms are most urgent in that part of the UN which deals with development. About 70% of the UN'S resources go into this field and 'extreme fragmentation of efforts' in almost every instance complicated the task of the developing countries rather than simplifying it.

The achievements of the present system are 'not negligible' and efforts made in the past four decades have clearly demonstrated the need for a world organization. But a 'crisis of the UN system' high-lighted by 'shortcomings of an unacceptable nature' has shown that a *thorough overhaul of the structure and an integrated answer to the problem of development is required.* (my emphasis)

(The above Report indicates the relevance of Regional Peace and Development Programmes as an ideal way of integrating development programmes within a structure of regional organization which would overcome the problems indicated in the UN Report.)

MEDIATION

'Agreement is needed between the nations in a region to resolve differences peacefully'. This is one of the key requirements included in the Code of Agreement. To assist this process the Proposal made by Professor Adam Curle for non-official Mediators could be helpful. The Proposal is made in his book *In the Middle: Non Official Mediation in Violent Situations*. (Bradford School of Peace Studies, Bradford, or from Berg Publishers). The quotation below is taken from the review of this book by Hendrik W. van der Merwe in the Quaker Journal *The Friend*:

Adam Curle, the well known and highly respected international mediator and first professor of the School of Peace Studies at Bradford, makes a convincing plea for non-official mediation as an effective means of persuading the warring factions in international conflict to agree to meet round the negotiating table.

For Adam Curle, mediation 'aims to remove largely psychological obstacles that prevent hostile parties coming together for constructive negotiation.' Mediation or conciliation is part of the process of reconciliation.

In the first section he discusses obstacles to peacemaking, focussing on 'anger, resentment and blind chauvinism that inhibit any moves towards peace', distorted perceptions mutual distrust and illusions.

In the next section he discusses non-official mediation as an effort 'to establish, or re-establish, sufficiently good communications between conflicting parties so that they can talk sensibly to each other without being blinded by such emotions as anger, fear and suspicions'.

While private, non-official mediators have no automatic entrée to recognised authority, have no political power and no resources and lack weight to achieve major diplomatic results, they may be seen by contending parties as being more impartial and honest than official diplomats who represent governments or other powerful bodies who may have vested interests. A major feature of this sort of mediation is its long duration, running into several years.

Mediators 'are trying to bridge with friendship the hate-filled gulf between people'. This friendship extends to both sides and may appear ambiguous to the protagonists. How can they trust people who claim to be on good terms with their sworn enemies? Mediators thus have to be constantly alert lest an unguarded word gives any suggestion of favouring the other side. 'It is only by unswerving truthfulness, friendliness and concerned impartiality that mediators earn the conditional right to be on good terms with both sides'.

In a section on *The Practice of Mediation* Adam Curle discusses four interwoven and overlapping aspects of the process:

1. Building, maintaining and improving communications.
2. Providing information.
3. Befriending.
4. Active mediation. By active mediation he refers to 'the more specifically diplomatic activity of mediators.'

While mediators do not promote particular approaches to the resolution of conflict they do participate in dialogue with a specific purpose, 'to argue strongly against the misunderstandings and preconceptions that strengthen these obstacles'. In order to illustrate this aspect of mediation the book contains twenty pages of dialogue of a mediator with a high government official and a guerrilla leader.

He deplores the fact that this kind of mediation is insufficiently developed and ends with a brief proposal for an International Mediation Centre. This would be set up as a non-governmental organization (NGO) having consultative status with the UN. It should identify situations where mediation was or might become desirable, train mediators and provide mediation teams.

The Charter of the United Nations

Chapter VIII Regional Arrangements. Article 52.

1. Nothing in the present Charter precludes the existence of regional arrangements or agencies for dealing with such matters relating to the maintainance of international peace and security as are appropriate for regional action, provided that such arrangements or agencies and their activities are consistent with the Purposes and Principles of the United Nations.

2. The members of the United Nations entering into such arrangements or constituting such agencies shall make every effort to achieve pacific settlement of local disputes through such regional arrangements or by such regional agencies before referring them to the Security Council.

3. The Security Council shall encourage the development of pacific settlement of local disputes through such regional arrangements or by such regional agencies either on the initiative of the States concerned or by reference from the Security Council.

4. This article in no way impairs the application of Articles 34 and 35.

Bibliography

Alternatives to War and Violence ed. Ted Dunn. A symposium of 24 essays. Clarke 1963.

Foundations of Peace and Freedom ed. Ted Dunn. A symposium of 27 essays. Christopher Davies (publisher) Ltd. 1975.

Proposal for World Peace Through Regional Peace and Development with Commendations by Ted Dunn and William Apps 1983 70p plus postage.

(The above three books are available from, 77, Hungerdown Lane, Lawford, Manningtree, Essex CO11 2LX)

From Marshall Plan to Global Interdependence. A series of addresses at a conference arranged to mark the occasion of the 30th anniversary of the Marshall Plan. Published by the Organisation for Economic Co-operation and Development, Paris. 1978.

Council of Europe Publications. Obtainable from H.M. Stationery Office, London, SE1, or from Council of Europe Publications, section 67006, Strasbourg Odex, France. The Council has a wide range of excellent information some free. *Forum* is their international journal. *The Catalogue of Publications* runs to 64 pages, dealing with human rights, law, crime, health, social co-operation, conservation, and education. Many studies are free.

United Nations Publications. Obtainable from H.M. Stationery Office, London SE1. Particularly relevant are:

The Brundtland Report. A Report of the UN Commission after studying the Environment and Development issues for three years. 1987.

The Relationship Between Disarmament and Development Study No 5.

Study of All the Aspects of Regional Development Study No 3.

Regional Co-operation—Report to the Secretary General 1986.

Development Forum—a monthly international newspaper published by the UN University.

United Nations Environment Programme. A Report of the *ad hoc* Expert Group Meeting on the Draft World Charter for Nature in 1981.

Vulnerability—Small States in a Global Society. A Report by a Commonwealth Consultative Group following the mandate given by Commonwealth Heads of States at their meeting in New Delhi. The Report recommends regional initiatives. Commonwealth Secretariat Publications. 1985.

The Establishment of an International Fund for Development. A Feasibility Study by Marek Thee of the International Peace Research Institute, Oslo. Financed by a grant from the UN Disarmament Project Fund.

The Foundations of Freedom. With special Reference to South Africa by D.V. Cowen, Professor of Comparative Law. Oxford University Press 1961. Should be compulsory reading for all concerned for S.A.

Lloyds Introduction to Jurisprudence by Lord Lloyd of Hampstead, Q.C. and M.D.A. Freeman LL.M. 'Now established as the leading text-book on the subject' Stevens. Fifth edition 1985.

The Theory of Justice by John Rawls, Professor of Philosophy Oxford University Press. 1983.

The Lawful Rights of Man. An Introduction to the International Legal Code of Human Rights by Paul Sieghart. Oxford University Press. 1986.

Alfred Russel Wallace. 'The great naturalist who challenged the orthodoxy which he and Darwin had established', by Harry Clements. Hutchinson. 1983.

Only One Earth, by Barbara Ward and Rene Dubas. Penguin 1972. The Unofficial Report of the UN Conference on the Human Environment held in Stockholm 1972.

Progress for a Small Planet, by Barbara Ward. Maurice Tempole Smith 1979. Also available in paperback by Penguin Book Ltd. 1979.

The Phenomenon of Man by Pierre Teilhard de Chardin. Fontana 1970.

Man's Place in Nature by Pierre Teilhard de Chardin. Fontana 1977.

North-South. A Programme for Survival (The Brandt Report) Pan Books 1980

Global Challenge. A Report of the Socialist International Committee on Economic Policy. Chaired by Michael Manley. Pan Books 1985

Education in Democracy. The Folk High Schools of Denmark by John Christmas Maller and Katherine Watson Faber and Faber 1944

Denmark: A Social Laboratory. Rural Development and the Changing Countries of the World. By Peter Manniche Pergamon Press Ltd. 1969.